THE CHARISMATIC THEOLOGY OF ST. LUKE

ROGER STRONSTAD

 HENDRICKSON
PUBLISHERS

TO
CLIFFORD STRONSTAD
and IRENE and ROBERT JONAS
and their daughters
JENNIFER and PAMELA
with affection

Scripture quotations are from the New American Standard Bible, © the Lockman Foundation 1960, 1962, 1963, 1971, 1972, 1973, 1975, 1977. Used by permission.

ISBN 0-913573-11-6

Eighth printing—February 2005

CONTENTS

ACKNOWLEDGMENTS

This present work is a revision of my Master's thesis which was submitted to Regent College in 1975. I wish to thank Dr. W. Ward Gasque, the supervisor of my research, for his model of careful scholarship and for his constructive comments. I am grateful to Dr. Clark H. Pinnock, my external examiner, for writing a generous Foreword to the book. Also, my thanks are due Dr. William Menzies, editor, for permission to incorporate in revised form material from my article, "The Influence of the Old Testament on the Charismatic Theology of St. Luke," *Pneuma*, Vol. 2, No. 1 (1980): 32–50.

It is my pleasant duty to express gratitude to those who helped me in the preparation of this manuscript; to Mrs. Carol Lutzke for typing the manuscript; to Miss Darleen Kifiak and Mrs. Colleen Daher for proofreading the manuscript, and Mr. Leonard Van Dyke for preparing the index to this manuscript. Above all, I am deeply grateful to my wife, Laurel, for her constant, patient, and loving support throughout this whole endeavor.

ROGER STRONSTAD

Clayburn, B. C., Canada
July, 1984.

FOREWORD

I am quite frankly excited at the appearance of Roger Stronstad's book *The Charismatic Theology of St. Luke*. Until now people have had to recognize Pentecostalism as a powerful force in the areas of spirituality, church growth, and world mission, but they have not felt it had much to offer for biblical, theological, and intellectual foundations. But this is fast changing, and with the appearance of this book we may be seeing the first motions of a wave of intellectually convincing Pentecostal theology which will sweep in upon us in the next decades. Watch out you evangelicals—the young Pentecostal scholars are coming! We are going to have to take them seriously in the intellectual realm as well as in the other areas. There can be no more looking down the nose at them from the unchallenged heights of superiority. Pentecostal theology will have to receive the respect which is already given to Lutheran, Calvinist, and Wesleyan thought. Pentecostal people can be proud of their new intellectual leaders, and assuming that they behave responsibly in their communities, I hope they will be given room to think and be affirmed in their calling. The Pentecostal experience deserves and needs a good theological articulation of the kind Roger offers us here.

I would further say that I think Roger is right in his position. St. Luke *does* support a charismatic theology and religion. Some of our best people, like Dale Bruner and James Dunn, have tried to impose their reading of Paul upon Luke's writings and have distorted it. Ironically, at this point at least, there is greater diversity in the New Testament than even Jimmy Dunn is prepared to grant! St. Luke speaks of a baptism of power for service which is not oriented to the soteriological work of the Spirit, which Paul often addresses. The theologies of Luke and Paul are complementary to each other but must not be confused as being identical in the usual way. Paul has room, of course, for what Luke says in his treatment of the charismatic structure of the congregation in 1 Corinthians 12–14, but Luke must not be imprisoned in one room of the Pauline house. Nor have we any right, as the custom is among evangelicals, to put Luke down because his work is narrative and not didactic theology. Stronstad clears up these confusions, as well as others, and gives us here a solid basis for Pentecostal thinking and practice.

The meaning of this book is that the walls must come down between Pentecostals and evangelicals. If canonical Luke has a charismatic theology as Stronstad proves, we cannot consider Pentecostalism to be a kind of aberration born of experiential excesses but a 20th century revival of New Testament theology and religion. It has not only restored joy and power to the church but a clearer reading of the Bible as well. So with gladness of heart I say, ''Welcome to this book and peace to the Pentecostal communities.'' We should let Stronstad help us grow together in the unity of the faith in the Son of God.

Clark H. Pinnock

McMaster Divinity College
Hamilton, Ontario.

CHAPTER ONE

The Holy Spirit in Luke-Acts: A Challenge in Methodology

For his lead essay in the *Festschrift* presented to Paul Schubert, W. C. van Unnik chose the title, "Luke-Acts, A Storm Center in Contemporary Scholarship."[1] As van Unnik chronicles Lukan scholarship in the '50s and '60s, this storm center includes among others the following subjects: 1) the relationship between the historical and theological character of Luke-Acts, 2) Luke's alleged shift from the expectation of an imminent parousia in the theology of the primitive church to a history of salvation theology, and 3) the differences between the Paul of the Acts and the Paul of the Epistles.[2] The publication of two benchmark books in 1970, *A Theology of the Holy Spirit* by Frederick Dale Bruner and *Baptism in the Holy Spirit* by James D. G.Dunn, however, added new winds of controversy to the storm center of Lukan scholarship; namely, the meaning of the activity of the Holy Spirit which is recorded in Luke-Acts.[3]

These winds of controversy rage most strongly over the interpretation of the "baptism in the Holy Spirit" which happened on the day of Pentecost and is used throughout the book of Acts. Traditionally, the Church has associated the baptism in the Holy Spirit with conversion and has identified it with incorporation into the body of Christ.[4] However, primarily beginning with John Wesley's seminal teaching on sanctification, Christians have increasingly challenged this interpretation. For example, holiness groups, emerging out of Methodism, "came to speak of entire sanctification as a 'baptism of the Holy Spirit'."[5] Moreover, Pentecostalism, the synthesis of late nineteenth century fundamentalist, dispensational, and holiness theology with camp meeting and revival methodology,[6] identified "baptism in the Holy Spirit" as an empowering for service. The sole distinctive element in Pentecostalism lies in its insistence that glossolalia is the essential evidence for the baptism in the Spirit.[7] Most recently, Charismatics, children of the marriage between Pentecostal experience and traditional Reformed, Lutheran, or Catholic theology, often interpret the baptism in the Holy Spirit to be a subsequent experiential actualization of the

1

Spirit who was given earlier in conversion/confirmation.[8] Thus, winds of division and controversy now sweep across current interpretations of the gift of the Holy Spirit in Luke-Acts.

This division is not simply theological. Fundamental hermeneutical or methodological differences lie at the heart of the matter. These methodological differences arise out of and are coextensive with the diverse literary genre of the New Testament. For example, Luke's theology of the Holy Spirit must be inferred from a two-volume "history" of the founding and growth of Christianity—of which volume one is classified as a Gospel and volume two is classified as the Acts.[9] In contrast, Paul's theology of the Holy Spirit must be derived from his letters, which he addressed to geographically separated churches at different times in his missionary career. These letters are circumstantial; that is, they are addressed to some particular circumstance: for example, news of controversy (Galatians), answers to specific questions (1 Corinthians), or plans for a forthcoming visit (Romans). Thus, while Luke *narrates* the role of the Holy Spirit in the history of the early church, Paul *teaches* his readers concerning the person and ministry of the Spirit.

It is this difference between narration and theology in the New Testament literature which raises the fundamental methodological issues for the doctrine of the Holy Spirit. Consequently, the experiential and theological tensions over the doctrine of the Holy Spirit will only be resolved when the methodological issues have first been resolved. Therefore, the following discussion focuses upon the methodological issues of the *crux interpretum* in the current debate: the meaning of the Holy Spirit in Luke-Acts.

In order to correctly interpret Luke's record of the Holy Spirit we must resolve three fundamental methodological problems: 1) the literary and theological homogeneity of Luke-Acts, 2) the theological character of Lukan historiography, and 3) the independence of Luke as a theologian.

1. The Literary and Theological Homogeneity of Luke-Acts

Though the canon of the New Testament separates them, Luke and Acts are a single two-volumed composition (Luke 1:1–4; Acts 1:1). Ending several decades of skepticism concerning the literary unity of these two books, W.C. van Unnik reports:

we speak of it [Luke-Acts] as a unit . . . . It is generally accepted that both books have a common author; the possibility that the Gospel and the Acts, contrary to Acts 1:1, do not belong together is not seriously discussed. By almost unanimous consent they are considered to be two volumes of a single work.[10]

This scholarly consensus on the literary unity of Luke-Acts has remained without serious challenge. In spite of this consensus concerning the literary unity of Luke-Acts, interpreters often assume that Luke-Acts reflects a theological discontinuity between its two parts, rather than a theological continuity or homogeneity.

Since the publication of *The Theology of St. Luke* (ET) in 1961, Hans Conzelmann has cast a long shadow across Lukan studies. The central feature of his theology is his peculiar, though popular, division of Lukan history into three epochs:

1. The period of Israel, of the Law and the Prophets;
2. The period of Jesus, which gives a foretaste of future salvation;
3. The period between the coming of Jesus and his Parousia, in other words, the period of the Church and of the Spirit. This is the last age. We are not told that it will be short.[11]

According to Conzelmann's interpretation, "There is continuity linking the three periods, and the essence of the one is carried through into the next."[12] Nevertheless, Conzelmann emphasizes that in Luke's theology there is "emphasis on the separation between the epochs."[13] Thus, as Conzelmann interprets Luke-Acts, he emphasizes the theological discontinuity between John the Baptist (the period of Israel), Jesus (the middle of time) and the epoch of the Spirit (the Church).[14]

The theological homogeneity of Luke-Acts is also denied on grounds other than the epochs of redemptive history. For example, in "The Holy Spirit in the Acts and the Fourth Gospel," W. F. Lofthouse asserts that the record of the Spirit in the Synoptic Gospels is "unable to act as a basis [for the Spirit] in Acts 1–15."[15] Rather, the basis for the portrayal of the Holy Spirit in Acts 1–15 is to be found in the teaching on the Spirit which is recorded in John 14–16.[16] Thus, according to Lofthouse's perspective, Luke's record of the activity of the Holy Spirit in Luke-Acts is influenced by two distinct traditions: 1) the Synoptic tradition for the Gospel, and 2) the Johannine tradition for the Acts of the Apostles. Amazingly, the Synoptic tradition about the Holy Spirit has no influence on the record of the Spirit in the Acts.

Not only is it commonplace to assert discontinuity between the successive pictures of the Holy Spirit in Luke-Acts, it is also commonplace to assert discontinuity even for the identical terminology which describes the Holy Spirit in Luke-Acts. For example, concerning the phrase "filled with the Holy Spirit" J. H. E. Hull writes:

Elizabeth and Zechariah were, in Luke's view, momentarily filled with the Spirit. In other words, they could only be aware of His (seemingly) fleeting presence and His (seemingly) fitful and necessarily limited activity. The disciples, on the other hand, were permanently filled with the Spirit.[17]

To undergird his exegetically baseless affirmation that the phrase "filled with the Holy Spirit" has a different (and superior?) meaning in Acts than it does in Luke, he changes the Lukan metaphor, writing:

As there is no indication that Elizabeth and Zechariah permanently possessed the gift of prophecy, we may say . . . that their experience of the Spirit was a momentary flash, illuminating them solely on the occasions referred to in the first chapter of Luke. As Acts suggests, however, the disciples' experience of the Spirit was, and continued to be, an all-consuming flame.[18]

The answer to Hull's distinction between the alleged temporary gift of the Spirit of prophecy to Elizabeth and Zechariah and the permanent gift of the Spirit of prophecy to the disciples is simply that for John the gift of the Spirit of prophecy was certainly permanent (Luke 1:15, 76; 20:6), and for the disciples it was demonstrably repetitive (Acts 2:4, 4:8, 31).

Conzelmann, Lofthouse, and Hull are three examples of the widespread tendency to emphasize the theological discontinuity between Luke and Acts. However, since Luke and Acts are a single work, it would be far more natural to stress their theological continuity or homogeneity. In fact, this proves to be the case. In *Luke: Historian and Theologian*, I. Howard Marshall demonstrates that important Lukan themes such as salvation, forgiveness, witness, and the Holy Spirit bind Luke-Acts together as one—albeit a two-volumed story.[19] He rightly observes:

What is significant is his [Luke's] combination of the story of Jesus and the story of the early church in one account. Thereby he testified that the two stories are really one, and that the break between them is not of such decisive importance as that between the period of the law and the prophets and the period in which the gospel of the kingdom is preached.[20]

On this issue of continuity/homogeneity or discontinuity between Luke and Acts, as the above examples illustrate, the balance is too often arbitrarily tipped in favor of discontinuity. Except where the evidence clearly leads elsewhere, the literary unity of Luke-Acts must compel the interpreter to recognize a theological homogeneity in the theology of the two books. This homogeneity is no less true for the charismatic theology of St. Luke than it is for his other distinctive doctrines and motifs.

2. The Theological Character of Lukan Historiography

Pentecostalism, and to a lesser extent its younger sibling, the Charismatic movement, has not only thrown down an experiential and theological challenge to contemporary Christianity, but it has also thrown down a fundamental methodological challenge. This challenge raises the question of the theological significance of Luke's narrative "history" of the activity of the Holy Spirit in the book of Acts. In interpreting the book of Acts, Pentecostals tend to emphasize the theological character of the narratives and de-emphasize their historical uniqueness. On the other hand, those who respond to their methodological challenge maximize the historical character of the narratives and minimize their theological character.

Upon five episodes in Acts, Pentecostals build their distinctive theology regarding the gift of the Spirit: 1) to the disciples on the day of Pentecost (2:1–13), 2) to the believers at Samaria (8:14–19), 3) to Saul of Tarsus (9:17–18), 4) to Cornelius and his household (10:44–46), and 5) to the disciples at Ephesus (19:1–7). In general terms, these "five events in the Book of Acts become the Biblical precedents of Spirit Baptism."[21] More specifically, "the events that occurred on the day of Pentecost are held to be the pattern for centuries to come,"[22] or that the Pentecost narrative establishes "the Scriptural pattern for believers of the whole church age."[23] As a natural corollary to their methodology, Pentecostals conclude:

On Biblical grounds, tongues are a necessary and essential evidence of baptism in the Spirit. . . God promised that the Biblical pattern was the standard for future times: "The promise is to you and to your children, and to all that are afar off" (Acts 2:38). What was true at the Day of Pentecost, and on subsequent occasions in Scripture, must continue to be true throughout the ages.[24]

Clearly, Pentecostals emphasize the "normative" theological intent of Luke's historical record of the gift of the Spirit for contemporary Christian experience.

Many interpreters, however, believe that this "Pentecost-as-Pattern" methodology violates the narratival or historical character of the book of Acts. For example, in his *Christianity Today* article, "Outburst of Tongues: The New Penetration," Frank Farrell writes:

> The few historical accounts of tongues in Acts, in comparison with the other Scriptures, provide a flimsy foundation indeed upon which to erect a doctrine of the Christian life; no directives for normative Christian experience are contained in these passages.[25]

In his widely influential book, *The Baptism and Fullness of the Holy Spirit*, John R. W. Stott expresses similar sentiments, writing:

> This revelation of the purpose of God in Scripture should be sought in its *didactic*, rather than its *historical* parts. More precisely, we should look for it in the teaching of Jesus, and in the sermons and writings of the apostles, and not in the purely narrative portions of the Acts.[26]

Later in his book Stott reiterates, "A doctrine of the Holy Spirit must not be constructed from descriptive passages in the Acts."[27] Farrell and Stott typify a methodological approach to Acts which drives a wedge between διδαχη (instruction) and narrative, between history and theology.

This criticism of the Pentecostal interpretation of Acts has forced Pentecostals to articulate a more sophisticated methodology for the descriptive, historical, or narrative passages in the Acts. [28] Their response to their critics, however, is not wholly convincing, for it concedes to their critics the legitimacy of the sharp and rigid distinction between history and διδαχη in New Testament literature. For example, in his pamphlet, *I'm Still There!*, Ronald Kydd concludes:

> I think such [historical] material may, and even should, be called upon when it meets the tests we've been talking about: that is, when the sequences of events in *historical* material is the only sequence in which events relating to that particular experience appear in Scripture and when *didactic* material does not modify the pattern observed in the historical material.[29]

Ironically, this new Pentecostal hermeneutic has wandered into the same methodological cul-de-sac as that previously trodden by their critics, namely, in alleging an unbiblical dichotomy between the so-called descriptive and didactic passages of Scripture.

While a full discussion of biblical historiography is beyond the scope of this investigation, this alleged distinction between description and διδαχη, it must be observed, is alien to the general New Testament understanding of biblical, that is, Old Testament historiography. For example, Paul incontestably perceived a didactic purpose in historical narrative. Including the historical literature of the Old Testament within his compass, he writes:

All Scripture is inspired by God and profitable for teaching (διδασκαλίαν) for reproof, for correction, for training in righteousness; that the man of God may be adequate, equipped for every good work (2 Timothy 3:16-17).

Similarly, he affirms, "For whatever was written in earlier times was written for our instruction (διδασκαλίαν)" (Romans 15:4). Thus, to cite but one example of Paul's methodology, the experience of Israel in the wilderness "happened to them as an example (τυπικως, and they were written for our instruction, upon whom ends of the ages have come" (1 Corinthians 10:11). If for Paul the historical narratives of the Old Testament had didactic lessons for New Testament Christians, then it would be most surprising if Luke, who modelled his historiography after the Old Testament historiography, did not invest his own history of the origin and spread of Christianity with a didactic significance.

As mentioned, the historical narratives of the Old Testament served as a model for Luke's historiography. In *Luke · Historian and Theologian,* I. Howard Marshall concludes, "The writings of Luke are plainly indebted to the Old Testament tradition."[30] Rather than modelling himself after the Hellenistic historiographer, "His style of writing, which is frequently reminiscent of the Septuagint, demands that he also be compared with Jewish historians."[31] In *Acts and the History of Earliest Christianity,* Martin Hengel carries this comparison between Luke and Jewish historians beyond Jewish biblical historians to Jewish intertestamental historians, writing:

A comparison of his [Luke's] work with that of Josephus or the books of the Maccabees, and here above all to II Maccabees, . . . shows his particular proximity to Jewish Hellenistic historiography. Luke is evidently influenced by a firm tradition with a religious view of history which essentially derives from the Septuagint. His imitation of the Septuagint shows that he wants quite deliberately to be in this tradition.[32]

Thus, Hengel correctly affirms that Luke, with the other Evangelists, "did have a theological interest which was at the same time a historical one."[33]

Having asked the question, "do history and theology stand in opposition to each other?"[34] Marshall answers:

Luke conceived his task as the writing of history and that we shall fail to do justice to his work if we do not think of him as a historian. Modern research has emphasized that he was a theologian . . . . His view of theology led him to write history.[35]

Therefore, since Luke has a theological interest, his narratives, though they are historical, are always more than simply descriptions or the record of "brute" facts.

Clearly, in Luke-Acts, both by what he includes or excludes from his record and by his actual description of events, Luke always gives an interpreted narration. As W.F. Lofthouse observes, "Whether we consider the narrative of Pentecost or any other references to the activity of the Spirit in Acts 1–15, we are clearly dealing with the interpretation of certain experiences."[36] Thus, the so-called *purely narrative portions* of the Acts prove to be a myth which has been created by the contemporary critic, rather than a legitimate evaluation of Lukan historiography.

In the light of Luke's indebtedness to both biblical and Jewish Hellenistic historiographers, and also the fact that his narratives are invariably an interpreted record of events, it is imperative that interpreters adopt a fresh methodological approach to the interpretation of the historical narratives in Luke-Acts. This approach must focus upon the actual nature of the narrative. Luke's narratives fall into a combination of one or more of the following four categories. They are 1) episodic, 2) typological, 3) programmatic, and/or 4) paradigmatic. In general, all of the narratives are episodic. In addition, a typological narrative is one that looks back to an historically analogous and relevant episode from earlier times, either in Luke-Acts or in the Old Testament. In contrast to the typological narrative, the essence of a programmatic narrative is that it points ahead to the unfolding of future events. Finally, a paradigmatic narrative is one that has normative features for the mission and character of God's people living in the last days.

To illustrate, Luke's inauguration narrative (Luke 3:1–4:44) has explicit typological elements—the rejection of Jesus by His own townspeople in Nazareth echoes Israel's earlier rejection of the charismatic prophets, Elijah and Elisha (Luke 4:22–30). Similarly, the Pentecost narrative (Acts 1:1–2:42) also has typological overtones—the transfer of the Holy Spirit from Jesus to the disciples reflects the earlier transfer of the Spirit from Moses to the seventy elders (Numbers 11:16–30). Moreover, just as the infancy narrative (Luke 1:5–2:52) is programmatic for the mission of Jesus to Israel, so the Pentecost narrative is programmatic for the mission of the disciples from Jerusalem to Judea to Samaria to the ends of the earth (Acts 1:8). Finally, just as the anointing of Jesus (Luke 3:22; 4:18) is a paradigm for the subsequent Spirit baptism of the disciples (Acts 1:5; 2:4), so the gift of the Spirit to the disciples is a paradigm for God's people throughout the "last days" as a charismatic community of the Spirit—a prophethood of all believers (Acts 2:16–21). Other narratives in Luke-Acts may or may not have all of these elements. Nevertheless, these episodic, typological, programmatic, and paradigmatic elements are the key to interpreting the historical-theological dimension of Lukan historiography.

In the light of these four narratival elements, the solution to Pentecostalism's methodological challenge is not to retreat behind an artificial and arbitrary "descriptive" vs. "didactic" dichotomy. Rather, it is to come to grips with the true nature of Luke's historiography. Deeply influenced by his biblical-septuagintal historiographical model, Luke narrates the story of the founding and growth of Christianity. As in his model, his episodes are historical-theological in intent. In other words, Luke never intended to give his readers a simple description of events, either to inform or to satisfy the curiosity of his readers about the origins of their faith. Therefore, however the details are to be worked out, in principle Luke's narratives are an important and legitimate data base for constructing a Lukan doctrine of the Spirit. Thus, rather than providing a flimsy foundation upon which to erect a doctrine of the Holy Spirit, as is commonly alleged, the historical accounts of the activity of the Spirit in Acts provide a firm foundation for erecting a doctrine of the Spirit which has normative implications for the mission and religious experience of the contemporary church.

3. The Theological Independence of Luke

The tendency to drive a wedge between διδαχη and historical narrative, which we have just reviewed, has led to an unfortunate corollary for the interpretation of the Holy Spirit in Luke-Acts. This corollary is the widespread belief that whereas we look to Luke for history we must turn to Paul for theology. As a result of this methodological program, Luke's data on the Holy Spirit are interpreted as though they were written by Paul. In *The Semantics of Biblical Language*, James Barr classifies this procedure as an "illegitimate identity transfer."[37] This Pauline interpretation of Luke is most evident for the characteristic Lukan phrases "baptized in the Holy Spirit" and "filled with the Holy Spirit."

In their *Christianity Today* article, "A Truce Proposal for the Tongues Controversy," Pinnock and Osborne speak for many interpreters when they write:

This [Pentecostal] argument is weak methodologically and exegetically. Didactic portions of Scripture must have precedence over historical passages in establishing doctrine. We ought to move here from the teaching of First Corinthians to the narrative of Acts rather than the reverse. When one follows this proper methodology, one notes that there is no manifestation of tongues which is normative.[38]

Authors of high caliber books on the Holy Spirit, such as Dunn, Green, and Stott, commonly adopt this faulty methodological approach to the teaching of Luke and Paul on the Holy Spirit.

Scholars typically define Luke's characteristic term "baptized in the Holy Spirit" according to Paul's meaning of the term. Instructing the church at Corinth, Paul writes, "For by one Spirit we were all baptized into one body, whether Jews or Greeks, whether slaves or free, and we were all made to drink of one Spirit" (1 Corinthians, 12:13). According to this metaphor, Spirit baptism "is the spiritual transformation which puts the believer 'in Christ', and which is the effect of receiving the gift of the Spirit (hence "baptism in the Spirit")."[39] Therefore, according to Paul, the metaphor signifies initiation and incorporation;[40] that is, "it is, in fact, the means of entry into the body of Christ."[41] Invariably, the references in Luke-Acts (Luke 3:16; Acts 1:5, 11:16) are given this Pauline meaning. Having surveyed the references to the baptism in the Holy Spirit in the New Testament, Stott writes:

> The Greek expression is precisely the same in all seven occurrences, and therefore *a priori*, as a sound principle of interpretation, it should refer to the same baptism experience in each verse.[42]

Consequently, when Luke reports this baptism of the Holy Spirit, by definition, it always and necessarily has the Pauline meaning.

Because in Pauline theology "baptism in the Holy Spirit" is always initiatory and incorporative, no alternative interpretation is admissable. Thus, we are told, "The Pentecostal arguments fall to the ground."[43] Similarly, we read, "So baptism with the Holy Spirit is not a second-stage experience for some Christians, but an initiatory experience for all Christians."[44] However, in a review of Michael Green's book, *I Believe in the Holy Spirit*, Clark Pinnock rightly observes:

> If you read Luke by himself, and listen to him, it seems rather clear that the outpouring of the Spirit he has in mind is not brought into relation to *salvation* [initiation/incorporation], as it is in Paul, but in relation to *service* and *witness*. Therefore, Luke does not tie the coming of the Spirit to the salvation event. . . . Even non-charismatics like Green, sensitive and open as they are to the renewal, seem unable to grant that the pentecostals may understand Acts better than they do.[45]

Similarly, Luke's phrase "filled with the Holy Spirit" is often defined or qualified by Paul's use of a similar one in Ephesians 5:18. He writes, "And do not get drunk with wine, for that is dissipation, but be filled with the Spirit.'' Though Luke uses the term nine times and Paul uses it but once,[46] Paul's use seems to be normative. For example, in *Baptism and Fullness of the Holy Spirit*, John R.W. Stott devotes a few random paragraphs to Luke's use of the term but devotes no less than nine pages to Paul's use of the term.[47] Again, Luke's very characteristic term is not only made to sound Pauline, but its importance is also subordinated to Paul's meaning of the term.

The methodology whereby Luke is read as though he were Paul presses him into the Pauline mold and strips him of his independence as a theologian in his own right. At the very least, as the following chart demonstrates, this methodology is absurd.

	Luke	Paul
Baptized in the Spirit	3x	1x
Filled with the Spirit	9x	1x

Of course, though theology is not to be reduced to mere statistics, it is strange, indeed, that in each case Paul's one use of the term should define Luke's majority use of the term. Since Luke's use of the terms "baptized" and "filled with the Spirit" differs from Paul's, then this *a priori* methodological program has effectively silenced his teaching on the doctrine of the Holy Spirit.

In regards to the general theological independence of Luke, I. Howard Marshall observes:

Luke was entitled to his own views, and the fact that they differ in some respects from those of Paul should not be held against him at this point. On the contrary, he is a theologian in his own right and must be treated as such.[48]

Therefore, since Luke is a theologian in his own right, interpreters ought to examine his writings with a mind open to the possibility that his perspective on the Holy Spirit may, in fact, differ from Paul's. Consequently, just as the recognition that Luke is a theologian as well as a historian makes Luke-Acts a legitimate data base for the doctrine of the Holy Spirit, so the recognition that Luke is independent of Paul will broaden the New Testament data base for the doctrine of the Holy Spirit. To recognize these two facts is to rehabilitate Luke as a historian-theologian of the Holy Spirit and to allow him to make a significant, unique, and independent contribution to the doctrine of the Holy Spirit.

Though it is a formidable challenge, the theological and methodological impasse in the contemporary church concerning the meaning of the

Holy Spirit in Luke-Acts is capable of being resolved. On the one hand, where it is appropriate, all parties in the current debate must abandon those largely self-serving methodological programs which conspire to either silence or to manipulate Luke's distinctive theology. On the other hand, all parties must develop a methodological consensus for interpreting the gift of the Spirit in Luke-Acts. At a minimum, this consensus must include the following principles: 1) Luke-Acts is theologically homogeneous, 2) Luke is a theologian as well as a historian, and 3) Luke is an independent theologian in his own right.

When Luke-Acts is interpreted in the light of this methodological program, Luke's message often proves to be radically different from some contemporary interpretations which are given to it. For example, contrary to some popular interpretations, Luke's characteristic phrase "filled with the Holy Spirit": 1) is modelled after its use in the Old Testament (LXX), 2) has the same meaning in the Gospel as it has in the Acts, and 3) has a different meaning in Luke-Acts than it has in Paul's Epistle to the Ephesians. In general terms, for Luke, the Holy Spirit is not brought into relation to salvation or to sanctification, as is commonly asserted, but is exclusively brought into relation to a third dimension of Christian life—service. Thus, when he is interpreted by the methodological program which we have discussed, Luke is found to have a charismatic rather than a soteriological theology of the Holy Spirit. This charismatic theology of the Spirit is no less valid for disciples in the twentieth century than it was for disciples in the first century.

CHAPTER TWO

Prolegomenon:
The Charismatic Spirit of God

The Hebrew and Greek Bibles influenced Luke's theology of the Holy Spirit in two fundamental ways: 1) important charismatic motifs, such as the transfer, sign, and vocational motifs, are reflected in Luke-Acts, and 2) the Septuagint, the Bible used by Luke and the early church, supplied Luke with the majority of the terms which he used to describe the activity of the Holy Spirit in New Testament times. In the light of this intimate relationship between the former and the latter records of the Spirit, the study of the charismatic activity of the Spirit of God is a necessary preliminary to a proper understanding of the Holy Spirit in Luke-Acts.

The subject of this chapter is specifically the charismatic activity of the Spirit of God, rather than a more general investigation of the word "spirit." As the standard lexicons remind us, both the Hebrew word *rûach* and the Greek word πνευμα originally meant "air in motion."[1] From this basic concept, these two words came to mean wind, breath, the human spirit, and the divine spirit. Connoting, as they do, invisibility, movement, power, and life, *rûach* and πνευμα were appropriate words to describe God in action. It is the idea of "God in action" which stands behind the biblical record of the charismatic activity of the Spirit of God.

The term "charismatic" must be distinguished from its contemporary meaning; that is, as it is used to describe the Neo-Pentecostal movement which penetrated the historical denominations of the '60s and '70s.[2] I use the term "charismatic" in a functional and dynamic sense. By "charismatic" I mean God's gift of His Spirit to His servants, either individually or collectively, to anoint, empower, or inspire them for divine service. As it is recorded in Scripture, therefore, this charismatic activity is necessarily an experiential phenomenon.

In discussing the charismatic activity of the Spirit of God, the Christian interpreter must resist the subtle temptation to interpret it in the light of his Christian knowledge. For example, in the *The Theological Wordbook of the Old Testament*, we read:

13

Context approves and the analogy of the NT strongly suggests that the *rûach* YHWH is the Holy Spirit, "in the fullest Christian sense" (A. F. Kirkpatrick, *Cambridge Bible, Psalms*, II, p. 293). From the outset God's *rûach* moves upon the primeval waters (Gen 1:2), "like a hypostasis or person" (H. Schultz, *Old Testament*, II, p. 184).[3]

In contrast to this view, in *The Spirit of God in the Old Testament* Lloyd Neve asks the question, "Is there any significant personalizing of the Spirit in the OT?"[4] and answers, "The final conclusion is overwhelmingly negative: there is no personalization of the Spirit within the limits of the OT."[5] Thus, in spite of the minority voice represented by the *Theological Wordbook*, in the Hebrew Bible the Spirit of God is neither fully personal nor the third member of the Trinity. These are Christian, not Hebrew, truths.

This study of the charismatic activity of the Spirit of God is divided into two parts. In part one, I investigate the charismatic Spirit in Old Testament times, and in part two, I investigate the charismatic Spirit in the Intertestamental period.

Part One: The Charismatic Spirit in Old Testament Times

The texts which describe the charismatic activity of the Spirit of God in Old Testament times are both historical and prophetic in character. I will investigate four aspects of these data: 1) the chronological distribution of the charismatic activity of the Spirit, 2) the septuagintal terminology which describes this charismatic activity, 3) the motifs which are characteristic of this activity of the Spirit, and 4) the prophetic anticipations for the charismatic activity of the Spirit in the coming age of restoration.

1. The Distribution of Charismatic Activity

The distribution of the charismatic activity of the Spirit of God in Israelite history is significant. This distribution is not homogeneous; that is, the Spirit of God is not regularly and consistently active throughout Israel's history. Neither is this distribution random. Rather, the charismatic activity of the Spirit of God falls into five clearly defined periods, which correspond to critical phases in the political and religious development of the nation. These periods of charismatic activity are: 1) the founding of the nation in the wilderness, 2) the period of the Judges, 3) the founding of the Monarchy, 4) the time of Elijah and Elisha, and 5) the period of Exile and Restoration.

The first concentrated outburst of charismatic activity is associated with the founding of the nation of Israel in the wilderness, and is characterized by a variety of functions. The workers who are charged with the preparation of Aaron's priestly garments or the building of the Tabernacle are endowed with craftsmanship skills through being filled with the Spirit of God (Exodus 28:3; 31:3; 35:31). Furthermore, as the political and spiritual leader of Israel, Moses has the Spirit upon him (Numbers 11:17). Moreover, when he divides his responsibilities with the seventy elders, the Lord puts his Spirit upon them as he had put it upon Moses (Numbers 11:25–29). Likewise, the enigmatic Balaam prophesies when the Spirit of God comes upon him (Numbers 23:5; 24:2). Finally, as heir apparent to Moses, Joshua, who earlier had received the Spirit in company with the elders, is subsequently filled with the Spirit (Numbers 27:18; Deuteronomy 34:9). And so, at the founding of Israel, the Spirit is active in a variety of roles, imparting craftsmanship skills, empowering leaders as individuals or as a group, and inspiring an itinerant nonIsraelite to prophesy.

The variety which characterized the charismatic activity of the Spirit at the founding of Israel is absent in the time of the Judges. In this chaotic and tragic period of Israel's early history the activity of the Spirit is restricted exclusively to the Judges. In times of national penitence God raised up Judges to deliver Israel from her oppressors. Many, though not all, of these Judges were charismatic. For example, the Spirit of the Lord came upon Othniel, "and he judged Israel" (Judges 3:10). In addition, the Spirit of the Lord came upon Gideon, Jephthah, and Samson (Judges 6:34; 11:29; 13:25; 14:6, 19; 15:14). These Judges, then, are charismatic warriors who have received military prowess through the gift of the Spirit.

The founding of the Monarchy to succeed the Judges is characterized by an outburst of charismatic activity focused upon Israel's first two kings, Saul and David. Complementing Samuel's anointing of Saul, the Spirit of the Lord comes upon him and he prophesies (1 Samuel 10:1–10). The Spirit of the Lord will come upon Saul two more times (1 Samuel 11:6; 19:23) and once upon his messengers (1 Samuel 19:20) before Saul loses his kingship to David. Just as the Spirit of the Lord had come upon Saul when Samuel anointed him, so the Spirit also came upon David when he was anointed by Samuel (1 Samuel 16:13; 2 Samuel 23:2). With David's descendants kingship in Israel becomes hereditary and loses the charismatic character which was evident in the anointing of Saul and David.

The mission to call Israel from its apostasy back to faithfulness to the Lord is dominated by those remarkable charismatic prophets Elijah and Elisha. A servant of Ahab's expects that the Spirit of the Lord will carry Elijah away, so that he will not be found (1 Kings 18:12). In turn, the sons of the prophets believe, "The Spirit of the Lord has taken him up and cast him on some mountain or into a valley" (2 Kings 2:16). Before Elijah is caught up into heaven, Elisha asks him that a double portion of his spirit be given to him (2 Kings 2:9). When Elisha returns to them, the sons of the prophets recognize that "the spirit of Elijah rests on Elisha" (2 Kings 2:15).

Finally, the Babylonian exile and subsequent restoration is also a time of charismatic activity. Of all the classical prophets, Ezekiel is most conscious of the power of the Spirit of the Lord in his life (Ezekiel 2:2; 3:12, 14, 24; 8:3; 11:1, 5, 24; 37:1; 43:5). Moreover, the post-exilic Chronicler consistently associates the gift of the Spirit with inspired speech, with particular emphasis on prophets and priests. This identification is made for the gift of the Spirit to Amasai (1 Chronicles 12:18), Jahaziel a Levite (2 Chronicles 20:14), and Zechariah the son of Jehoiada the priest (2 Chronicles 24:20). In retrospect, it was recognized that the Spirit had also been given to Israel to instruct them (Nehemiah 9:20) and to witness to them (Nehemiah 9:30).

Having outlined this chronological distribution of the charismatic activity of the Spirit of God, we can now draw some conclusions about its significance. First, the offices which correspond to the five periods of Israel's political and religious development are charismatic. In Moses, Joshua, and the elders, the fledgling nation has its founding fathers; in Othniel, Gideon, and others, the tribal society has its charismatic warriors; in Saul and David, the tribal confederation has its charismatic kings; in Elijah and Elisha, an apostate Israel has its charismatic prophets; and in Ezekial and Zechariah, the son of Jehoiada the priest, Judah during the Exile and Restoration has its charismatic prophets and priests. With few exceptions, then, the charismatic activity of the Spirit of God is successively concentrated upon founding fathers, Judges, Kings, Prophets, and Priests.

Second, there is no experiential continuity between these five periods of the charismatic activity of the Spirit. With the exception of the time of the Judges, these periods of charismatic activity are clearly defined chronologically and are separated by gaps of up to two centuries or more. The texts demonstrate that the cessation of the charismatic experience in any one period is never permanent or irrevocable. The nation can always anticipate a future outpouring of the Spirit, such as the prophets predict for the coming age of the Messiah. Because it is Israel's God who gives his Spirit at these key periods of its political and religious development, the continuity rests in him and not in the recipients of the Spirit.

Third, the descriptions of the charismatic activity of the Spirit are typically programmatic. The examples of Moses and Elijah illustrate this principle. The reader of the Exodus and Wilderness narratives would be ignorant of Moses' charismatic leadership apart from the description in Numbers 11 of the transfer of the Spirit from Moses to the elders of Israel. There we read:

"Then I will come down and speak with you there, and I will take of the Spirit who is upon you, and will put *Him* upon them; and they shall bear the burden of the people with you, so that you shall not bear it alone." Then the Lord came down in the cloud and spoke to him; and He took of the Spirit who was upon him and placed *Him* upon the seventy elders. And it came about that when the Spirit rested upon them, they prophesied. But they did not do *it* again (Numbers 11:17, 25).

This narrative implies what is not recorded elsewhere—Moses administered Israel by the power of the Spirit.

The same is also true for Elijah. Apart from the record of the transfer of the Spirit from Elijah to Elisha, the reader would not know that either of these prophets were charismatic. Yet Elisha requests a double portion of Elijah's spirit (2 Kings 2:9), and the sons of the prophets recognize that the spirit of Elijah rested upon Elisha. With remarkable economy, this record of the transfer of the Spirit informs the reader of the charismatic ministry which Elijah exercised and at the same time anticipates the charismatic ministry of Elisha.

This same economy is evident for men such as Joshua, Samson, Saul, and others. Evidently, none of the biblical narrators ever felt that it was necessary to make explicit every example of charismatic activity. They appear to have been content to give programmatic descriptions of a charismatic ministry which was far greater than a statistical count of these narratives would imply.

2. Septuagintal Terminology

While the charismatic motifs are the same whether they are derived from either the Hebrew or the Greek Bible, because many of the biblical quotations in Luke-Acts reflect the septuagintal text, the septuagintal terminology which describes the charismatic activity of the Spirit merits

special study. The translators of the Septuagint used many verbs to
describe the charismatic activity of the Spirit. They are listed in order of
increasing frequency.

1. I bear witness (ἐπίμαρτυρεω, aor., 1x), Neh 9.29.
2. I carry (πορευομαι, aor., 1x), Ezek 3:14.
3. I cast (ῥιπτω, aor., 1x) 2 Kings 2:16.
4. I depart (ἀφιστημι, aor., 1x), 1 Sam 16:14.
5. I fall upon (πιπτω ...ἐπι, aor., 1x) Ezek 11:5.
6. I go out with (συνεκπορευομαι, aor., 1x) Judg 13:25.
7. I take from (ἀφαιρεω, fut, 1x), Num 11:17.
8. I come upon (ἐρχομαι ... ἐπι, aor., 2x), Ezek 2:2; 3:24.
9. I have (ἐχω, pres., 2x), Gen 41:38; Num 27:18.
10. I lift up (ἐξαιρω, aor., 2x), Ezek 2:2; 3:14.
11. I put upon (ἐπιτιθημι, fut/aor., 2x), Num 11:17, 25.
12. I raise (αἱρω, aor., 2x), 1 Kings 18:12; 2 Kings 2:16.
13. I speak (λεγω, aor., 2x), Ezek 3:24; 11:5.
14. I stand (ἱστημι, aor., 2x), Ezek 2:2; 3:24.
15. I talk (λαλεω, aor., 2x), 2 Sam 23:2; Ezek 3:24.
16. I clothe (ἐνδυω, aor., 3x), Judg 6:34; 1 Chron 12:18; 2 Chron 24:20.
17. I give (διδωμι, aor., 3x), Num 11:29; Neh 9:20; Isa 42:1.
18. I fill (ἐμπιμπλημι, aor., 4x), Exod 28:3; 31:3; 35:31; Deut 34:9.
19. I rest upon (ἐπαναπαυω ... επι, aor., 4x), Num 11:25–26; 2 Kings 2:15; Isa 11:2.
20. I lead (ἀγω, aor., 5x), Ezek 8:3; 11:1, 24; 37:1; 43:5.
21. I come/leap upon (/ἐφ/αλλομαι, aor., 7x), Judg 14:6, 19; 1 Sam 10:6, 10; 11:6; 16:13.
22. I take up (ἀναλαμβανω, aor., 7x), Ezek 2:2; 3:12, 14; 8:3; 11:1, 24; 43:5.
23. I come upon (γινομαι ... ἐπι, aor., 9x), Num 23:6; 24:2; Judg 3:10; 11:29; 1 Sam 19:20, 23; 2 Kings 2:9; 2 Chron 15:1; 20:14.

The texts seldom have man as the subject. When they do, man is said
to have (ἐχω) the Spirit. Joseph and Joshua are said to have the Spirit in
(ἐν) them (Genesis 41:38, Numbers 27:18). This is a characteristic state
or condition, for the verb "to have" is typically in the present tense.

The texts which have God as the subject are more numerous than
those which have man as the subject. God is the subject of several
different verbs. For example, he filled (πιμπλημι, aor., 4x) the crafts-
men with the Spirit of wisdom and Joshua with the Spirit of knowledge

(Exodus 28:3; 31:3; 35:31, Deuteronomy 34:9). In addition, the Lord promises to take (ἀφαιρεω) the Spirit from upon (ἐπι) Moses and put (ἐπιτιθημι) it upon (ἐπι) the elders (Numbers 11:17), an event which is subsequently described by verbs in the aorist tense (Numbers 11:25). Furthermore, the Lord gave/put (διδωμι, aor., 3x) the Spirit upon (ἐπι) the elders, to Israel, and upon his servant Jacob/Israel (Numbers 11:29; Nehemiah 9:20; Isaiah 42:1).

The texts with the Spirit as the subject use the widest variety of verbs to describe the charismatic activity of the Spirit. The Spirit rested upon (ἐπαναπαυω . . . ἐπι, 4x) the elders, Elisha, and the Scion of David (Numbers 11:25–26; 2 Kings 2:15; Isaiah 11:2). The Spirit also came upon (γινομαι . . .ἐπι, aor., 9x) Balaam, Othniel, Jephthah, the messengers whom Saul sent to David, Saul himself, Elisha, Azariah, and Jahaziel (Numbers 23:6; 24:2, Judges 3.10; 11·29, 1 Samuel 19:20, 23; 2 Kings 2:9, 2 Chronicles 15:1; 20:14). In addition, the Spirit clothed (ἐνδυω, aor., 3x) Gideon, Amasai, and Zechariah the son of Jehoiada (Judges 6:34, 1 Chronicles 12:18, 2 Chronicles 24:20). Moreover, the Spirit of the Lord came mightily upon (ἡλατο . . . ἐπι, 7x) Samson, Saul, and David (Judges 14:6, 19; 15:14; 1 Samuel 10:6, 10; 11:6; 16:13). Finally, the Spirit of the Lord spoke (λαλεω, 2x; λεγω, 1x) by David and to Ezekiel (2 Samuel 23:2, Ezekiel 2:2; 3:24).

The Spirit is remarkably prominent in Ezekiel where a variety of verbs, often in combination, describe the action of the Spirit. For example, Ezekiel reports that "the Spirit entered me and set me on my feet" (Ezekiel 2:2). In order of increasing frequency, the Spirit carried Ezekiel (πορευομαι, aor., 1x), fell upon him (πιπτω, aor., 1x), lifted him up (ἐξαιρω, aor., 2x), stood him upon his feet (ἱστημι, aor., 2x), came upon him (ἐρχομαι . . . ἐπι, aor., 2x), led him (ἀγω, aor., 5x), and took him up (ἀναλαμβανω, aor., 7x).

It is not always clear whether this terminology in Ezekiel describes a visionary experience or whether it describes a physical phenomenon. However, similar language is used for Elijah in a non-visionary context. It is expected that the Spirit can raise Elijah (αἰρω, aor., 2x) and cast him (ῥιπτω, aor., 1x) into the Jordan (1Kings 18:12, 2 Kings 2:16).

Two other verbs are used one time to describe the activity of the Spirit. The Spirit began to stir Samson (συνεκπορευεσθαι), (Judges 13:25) and the Spirit departed (ἀπεστη) from Saul (1 Samuel 16:14).

In summary, in order to describe the complex character of the charismatic activity of the Spirit of God, the narrators use a multitude of

terms, amounting to over twenty verbs in the Septuagint. Though man
may have the Spirit, and God may either fill with the Spirit, take/put, or
give the Spirit, most often the Spirit acts directly. Typically, the Spirit
acts upon (ἐπι), though occasionally in/by (ἐν) or to (προσ), some
individual or group. Almost without exception, the translators use the
aorist tense to describe this charismatic activity of the Spirit, thereby
emphasizing the historical act rather than a condition or a state.

3. Charismatic Motifs

A. The Transfer Motif

The most striking motif for the charismatic activity of the Spirit of
God is the transfer of the Spirit in association with the transfer of
leadership. In the context of the programmatic character of the narratives, we have already referred to the transfer of the Spirit from Moses
to the elders and from Elijah to Elisha. In addition, there is also a
transfer of the Spirit from Moses to Joshua, and from Saul to David.
This transfer of the Spirit has a twofold purpose: 1) to authenticate or
accredit the new leadership, and 2) to endow the appropriate skills for
the new leadership responsibilities.

The first recorded transfer of leadership is from an individual to a
group—from Moses to the seventy elders (Numbers 11:10–30). After
one in a series of continuing complaints by Israel, Moses protests to the
Lord, "I alone am not able to carry all this people, because it is too
burdensome for me" (Numbers 11:14). In response to Moses' protest,
the Lord instructs him, "Gather for Me seventy men from the elders of
Israel" (Numbers 11:16). He then promises, "I will take of the Spirit
who is upon you, and will put *Him* upon them; and they shall bear the
burden of the people with you" (Numbers 11:17). When Moses and the
elders have gathered at the Tabernacle:

Then the Lord came down in the cloud and spoke to him; and He took of the Spirit who
was upon him and placed *Him* upon the seventy elders. And it came about that when the
Spirit rested upon them, they prophesied. But they did not do *it* again (Numbers 11:25).

In this and subsequent examples, the transfer of the Spirit is the necessary complement to the transfer of the responsibility of leadership.

After a generation in the wilderness, the imminent death of Moses
makes it imperative to appoint a successor to lead Israel into the promised land. So that at his death Israel will not be as "sheep without a

shepherd,'' Moses requests the Lord to ''appoint a man over the congregation'' (Numbers 27:16). The Lord then instructs Moses:

Take Joshua the son of Nun, a man in whom is the Spirit, and lay your hand on him. And you shall put some of your authority on him; in order that all the congregation of the sons of Israel may obey *him* (Numbers 27:18–20).

A parallel passage in Deuteronomy looks back to this incident:

Now Joshua the son of Nun was filled with the spirit of wisdom, for Moses had laid his hands on him; and the sons of Israel listened to him and did as the Lord had commanded Moses (Deuteronomy 34:9).

This latter text makes explicit what was implied in the earlier text. The transfer of leadership from Moses to Joshua is accompanied by the corresponding transfer of the Spirit.

With Saul and David the reader encounters a further example of the transfer of both leadership and the Spirit. When Samuel anointed Saul to be king, ''the Spirit of God came upon him mightily'' (1 Samuel 10:10). In identical fashion, when Samuel anointed David to be Saul's successor, ''the Spirit of the Lord came mightily upon David from that day forward'' (1 Samuel 16:13). That this is a true transfer of the Spirit from Saul to David is confirmed by the fact that having come upon David, ''the Spirit of the Lord departed from Saul'' (1 Samuel 16:14).

The transfer of the Spirit from Elijah to Elisha is a further example of this recurring motif. The text reports, ''Elijah said to Elisha, 'Ask what I shall do for you before I am taken from you.' And Elisha said, 'Please, let a double portion of your spirit be upon me' '' (2 Kings 2:9). This request is soon fulfilled, for the sons of the prophets recognize that ''The spirit of Elijah rests on Elisha'' (2 Kings 2:15). This transfer of the prophetic vocation and the gift of the Spirit is confirmed by Elisha's ability to part the Jordan river just as Elijah had done earlier (2 Kings 2:8,14).

B. The Sign Motif

The description of Saul's anointing clearly states that one purpose of the gift of the Spirit is to give a sign (σημειον) to confirm or authenticate God's call to leadership. Samuel tells Saul that a sign will confirm ''that the Lord [has] anointed you a ruler over His inheritance'' (1 Samuel 10:1). He then enumerates three signs that will come to Saul: 1) at Rachel's tomb he will learn that the lost asses have been found,

2) at Bethel he will be given two loaves of bread, and 3) at Gibeah the Spirit of God will come upon him and he will prophesy (1 Samuel 10:2–6). With special emphasis on the third sign, the text reports that

all those signs came about on that day. When they came to the hill there, behold, a group of prophets met him; and the Spirit of God came upon him mightily, so that he prophesied among them. And it came about, when all who knew him previously saw that he prophesied now with the prophets, that the people said to one another, "What has happened to the son of Kish? Is Saul also among the prophets?" (1 Samuel 10:9b–11).

This narrative makes it clear that the gift of the Spirit of prophecy, on the one hand, gives Saul the experiential confirmation or sign that God is with him (1 Samuel 10:7) and, on the other hand, publicly demonstrates to the nation that Saul is the Lord's anointed.

For Saul, the gift of the Spirit of prophecy may function as but one sign among others, but this sign is also observable in several other narratives. For example, the transfer of leadership from Moses to the elders and the complementary gift of the Spirit reflects a similar pattern. At the beginning of their new leadership responsibilities, the Spirit is placed upon the elders and they prophesy. Moreover, the gift of the Spirit to David at his anointing is described in identical terms to the earlier gift to Saul, authenticating him as the divinely chosen successor to Saul. Whereas no sign is recorded when the Spirit comes upon him, like his predecessor David, he is also a prophet. In a later text he claims, "The Spirit of the Lord spoke by me, and His word was on my tongue" (2 Samuel 23:2).

In addition to the explicit sign function of the prophetic dimension of the gift of the Spirit, there is also a general association of the gift of the Spirit and prophecy. In Chronicles, for example, the texts follow an invariable pattern: the description of the gift of the Spirit is always followed by a report of direct speech. This pattern is evident for Amasai, Azariah the son of Obed, Jahaziel a Levite, and Zechariah the son of Jehoiada the priest (1 Chronicles 12:18, 2 Chronicles 15:1; 20:14; 24:20). This pattern, which implies prophetic inspiration for those who are not prophets by office, is also evident in prophets such as Balaam and Ezekiel (Numbers 23:6 LXX; Ezekiel 11:5). And so, whether the evidence comes from the experience of Saul, the seventy elders, the writings of the Chronicler, or elsewhere, the prophetic gift of the Spirit always has an experiential and functional dimension, a dimension which in some cases, at least, serves as an explicit sign to authenticate or confirm God's call to service.

C. The Vocational Motif

The gift of the Spirit is not only a sign to confirm God's call, it also endows skills which are appropriate for this call to leadership. For example, God fills the artisans who make Aaron's priestly garments or who work on the Tabernacle with "the spirit of perception" (Exodus 28:3, LXX) or with "a divine spirit of wisdom and understanding" (Exodus 31:3; 35:31, LXX). For these artisans, the spirit of wisdom is the Spirit who imparts wisdom, a wisdom which is manual skill or craftsmanship. Similarly, as successor to Moses, Joshua is "filled with the spirit of knowledge" (Deuteronomy 34:9, LXX). In contrast to the spirit of wisdom and understanding as craftsmanship, for Joshua the spirit of understanding is the ability to lead a typically disobedient and wayward nation into the promised land.

The gift of the Spirit to the Judges imparts military prowess rather than craftsmanship or leadership. The first Judge, Othniel, illustrates this dimension of the gift of the Spirit. We read, "The Spirit of the Lord came upon him, and he judged Israel. When he went out to war, the Lord gave Cushanrishathaim king of Mesopotamia into his hand" (Judges 3:10). This same gift of military prowess is also evident for Gideon (Judges 6:34), Jephthah (Judges 11:29), and in a modified way for Samson (Judges 13:25ff). Samson's unique characteristic as Judge is his physical strength imparted by the gift of the Spirit. Three times it is reported of him that "the Spirit of the Lord came upon him mightily" (Judges 14:6, 19; 15:14).

Dissatisfied with their inability to cope with the Philistine menace, the people force Samuel to institute the monarchy, demanding, "Now appoint a king for us to judge us like all the nations" (1 Samuel 8:5). In contrast to the village and tribal society of the Judges, the monarchy will involve: 1) a standing army, 2) a centralized authority with its bureaucracy, and 3) a dynastic succession. Nevertheless, the narrator describes kingship in language which deliberately echoes the role of the Judges. For example, at their anointing by Samuel, the Spirit of the Lord came mightily upon Saul and David—a description which echoes the gift of the Spirit to Samson. Therefore, while the reigns of Saul and David represent a radical political and social break with the era of the Judges, the narrator still casts them in the role of charismatic warriors so characteristic of their predecessors.

This survey of the charismatic activity of the Spirit of God has illustrated three closely related themes or motifs. At key periods in Israel's

history the transfer of leadership, or even the independent call to leadership, is typically accompanied by a complementary transfer or gift of
the Spirit. This gift of the Spirit to Israel's leaders often has an experiential dimension, such as the manifestation of prophecy, to serve as
a sign to confirm God's call. Not only is this charismatic activity experiential, but it is also functional, for it also endows skills appropriate
for this call to leadership and service. In summary, these charismatic
motifs describe the gift of the Spirit of God to His people for divine
service or vocation.

4. The Spirit in the Messianic Age

Thus far we have limited our discussion to the historical record of the
charismatic activity of the Spirit of God. Yet there is also a prophetic
anticipation for the gift of the Spirit in the coming age when God will
visit His people and restore their fortunes. This activity of the Spirit is
concentrated upon a unique charismatic leader and a people who are
both empowered and renewed by the Spirit.

The prophet Isaiah describes the gift of the Spirit to an enigmatic
leader. In describing this leader as "a shoot . . . from the stem of
Jesse" (Isaiah 11:1), the prophet establishes the leader's Davidic
lineage. He then continues:

And the Spirit of the Lord will rest on Him,
The spirit of wisdom and understanding,
The spirit of counsel and strength,
The spirit of knowledge and the fear of the Lord
(Isaiah 11:2).

In a later text the Lord puts His Spirit upon His servant, proclaiming

Behold, My Servant, whom I uphold;
My chosen one *in whom* My soul delights.
I have put My Spirit upon him;
He will bring forth justice to the nations
(Isaiah 42:1).

A final text seems to describe the experience of the prophet himself. He
claims:

The Spirit of the Lord God is upon me,
Because the Lord has anointed me—
To bring good news to the afflicted;
He has sent me to bind up the broken-hearted,
To proclaim liberty to captives,
and freedom to prisoners (Isaiah 61:1).

Whatever difficulties the tension in these texts between the royal and prophetic offices, the individual and corporate character of the servant, and the present and future aspect of the Lord's anointing creates for the interpreter, one fact stands clear: these texts describe a charismatic leader—the Lord's anointed, the Messiah.

This charismatic gift of the Spirit of the Lord to the Messiah has a twofold significance. First, it signifies that his ministry is not simply hereditary; that is, a matter of royal or dynastic succession. Like David himself, he will fill his office by right of divine call. He expresses the consciousness of his call in the claim, "And now the Lord God has sent Me, and His Spirit" (Isaiah 48:16). In fact, the gift of the Spirit gives the Messiah a status unequalled among either David's sons or the prophets, for it puts him in the tradition of Israel's great charismatic founders—Moses, Joshua, and David.

Second, the gift of the Spirit to the Messiah, as for his charismatic predecessors, equips him with the skills appropriate for his call. It is fitting that for his unparalleled mission he receives the fullest endowment of the Spirit which is recorded in Scripture: the sixfold Spirit of wisdom and understanding, counsel and strength, and knowledge and the fear of the Lord. The programmatic character of the prophet's descriptions of the gift of the Spirit to the Messiah naturally results in a numerically small corpus of texts. Though they are few in number, they indicate that, in comparison to any of Israel's charismatic leaders, the Messiah is uniquely a man of the Spirit.

In the coming age, however, the Spirit will not rest exclusively upon the Messiah. Rather, he will share the charismatic gift of the Spirit with the restored people of God. In the prophet Joel we meet the vision of a widespread charismatic or prophetic ministry. His now classic oracle reads:

And it will come about after this
That I will pour out My Spirit on all mankind;
And your sons and daughters will prophesy,
Your old men will dream dreams,
Your young men will see visions.
And even on the male and female servants
I will pour out My Spirit in those days
(Joel 2:28–29).

As Joel predicts it, this outpouring of the Spirit is for all mankind, which in context means all Israel. In pouring out His Spirit upon the nation, God will give the Spirit of prophecy to young men as well as to elders, to daughters, and even to slaves. In revolutionary terms, the prophet announces that when God visits His people to restore their fortunes, the Spirit of prophecy will no longer be restricted to Israel's leaders, nor given in conformity to the norms of Israelite society. Instead, it will be universal both in extent and status. This future outpouring of the Spirit upon the Lord's anointed and upon His people will create a charismatic community.

Complementing this creation of a future charismatic community, God will also create a new Israel through the inward renewal of the Spirit. Using a wide range of metaphors and allusions, the prophets Isaiah and Ezekiel give voice to this hope. The renewal of the Spirit is described in terms of the cleansing or purifying action of water and fire, on the one hand, and the breath of life, on the other hand (Isaiah 4:4, Ezekiel 37:5–6). It will also be like the life-giving rain in the desert (Isaiah 44:3). Moreover, this inward renewal will necessitate a new covenant:

"As for me, this is My covenant with them," says the Lord: "My Spirit which is upon you, and My words which I have put in your mouth, shall not depart from your mouth, nor from the mouth of your offspring, nor from the mouth of your offspring's offspring," says the Lord, "from now and forever" (Isaiah 59:21).

Finally, God guarantees the effectiveness of this new covenant by promising Israel:

"Moreover, I will give you a new heart and put a new spirit within you; and I will remove the heart of stone from your flesh and give you a heart of flesh. And I will put My Spirit within you and cause you to walk in My statutes, and you will be careful to observe My ordinances" (Ezekiel 36:26–27).

In summary, as the prophets describe it, the gift of the Spirit of God in the age to come will be characterized by two new dimensions. In the first place, God will pour out His Spirit on a universal scale. Certainly the community of the new age will have a uniquely chosen, equipped, and sent charismatic leader, but for the first time the community itself will be charismatic. The difference between the charismatic activity of the Spirit throughout Israelite history and the age to come is one of magnitude; the gift of the Spirit to individuals or groups will give way to the gift of the Spirit to the community.

In the second place, in the age to come God's people will experience a totally new dimension of the Spirit—the indwelling of the Spirit. By His Spirit God will cleanse and purify His people from their sins, create new life in them, and impart to them the ability to keep His covenantal demands. The inward renewal of the Spirit, which results from the indwelling of the Spirit, complements the charismatic gift of the Spirit. With God pouring out His Spirit upon them, the future community of the Lord's anointed will receive both charismatic and moral or spiritual power.

Part Two: The Charismatic Spirit in the Intertestamental Period

The Judaism of the intertestamental period differs in many ways from the life of biblical Israel. Historically, the waxing and waning of empires—Persian, Greek, and Roman—continues its inexorable movement across the landbridge between Asia, Europe, and Africa, which in the south is the *eretz* Israel, the homeland of the Jews. Though the Judaism of the intertestamental period remains firmly rooted in its biblical faith, the intermingling of these diverse oriental and occidental influences irreversibly turns Judaism down uncharted historical, cultural, and theological paths.

Like a giant centrifuge, the Imperial forces of dispersion, which began with the Assyrian and Babylonian exiles, continue to propel God's people to new and distant lands—Asia Minor, Europe, Egypt, and northern Africa. As a result of this dispersion, Aramaic increasingly displaces Hebrew as the language of the Jews, to be partially displaced, in turn, by Greek. Thus it is in Alexandria, Egypt that the Hebrew Bible is first translated into the Greek language (ca. 250–150 B.C.). Moreover, latent biblical truths develop into full-fledged doctrines: for example, dualism, angelology, demonology, and the resurrection of the dead. Theologically, however, one of the most important differences between the faith of Israel and that of Judaism is negative: the self-conscious awareness of the loss of prophetic inspiration from the former to the latter period.

1. The Cessation of Prophetic Inspiration

In contrast to the Hebrew Bible, the classical literature of the intertestamental period is singularly devoid of the charismatic, vocational, and experiential activity of the Spirit of God. Several widely scattered texts toward the close of this period eloquently witness to the belief in the cessation of charismatic activity, in general, and prophetic inspiration, in particular. For example, the pseudonymous author of II Baruch laments:

But now the righteous have been gathered
And the prophets have fallen asleep,
And we also have gone forth from the land,

And Zion has been taken from us,
And we have nothing now save the Mighty One
and His law (2 Baruch 85:3).

Similarly, the Jewish apologist and historian, Josephus, gives formal expression to this belief in the cessation of prophetic inspiration. In *Against Apion* he writes:

From Artaxerxes to our own time the complete history has been written, but has not been deemed worthy of equal credit with the earlier records, because of the failure of the exact succession of the prophets (I. 41).

Finally, a late rabbinic tradition explains:

When the last prophets, Haggai, Zechariah, and Malachi, died, the holy spirit ceased out of Israel; but nevertheless it was granted them to hear (communications from God) by means of a mysterious voice (Tos Sot 8:2).[6]

These texts, therefore, consistently witness to the widespread conviction in the intertestamental period that prophetic inspiration had ceased in the past.

The cessation of prophetic inspiration has two important consequences for the religious literature of the intertestamental period. First, it established the temporal boundary dividing biblical literature from the Apocrypha and Pseudepigrapha. Nothing which had been written later than Malachi could be biblical, because *ipso facto* it could not be inspired. Second, it gave impetus to a significant body of pseudonymous literature. With the cessation of prophetic inspiration one could not write authoritatively in his own name but now had to write pseudonymously; that is, in the name of biblical heroes such as Enoch, the Twelve Patriarchs, Baruch, and Ezra.

2. The Restoration of Prophetic Inspiration

Conscious of the absence of prophetic inspiration, Judaism looked ahead to the future restoration of prophecy in Israel. For example, as part of the purification of the Temple, which Judas Maccabeus had just recaptured from the Syrians (December, 164 B.C.), the priests "tore down the altar, and stored the stones in a convenient place on the temple hill until there should come a prophet to tell them what to do with them" (1 Maccabees 4:46). Later, the Jews appointed Simon, the brother of Judas, "leader and high priest for ever, until a trustworthy prophet should arise" (1 Maccabees 14:44).

When pro-Hasmonean sentiment peaked in the golden age of Maccabean rule under John Hyrcanus (134–04 B.C.), his supporters believed that prophecy was restored in him. Josephus records this conviction:

> He was the only man to unite in his person three of the highest privileges: the supreme command of the nation, the high priesthood, and the gift of prophecy. For so closely was he in touch with the Deity, that he was never ignorant of the future; thus he foresaw and predicted that his two elder sons would not remain at the head of affairs (*Jewish War*, I. 68–69).

The belief that the Hasmonean priest-rulers also had the gift of prophecy surfaces in the pro-Hasmonean piece of propaganda, the *Testament of Levi*. In a vision Levi is commanded, "Arise, put on the robe of priesthood, and the crown of righteousness . . . and the ephod of prophecy" (8:2–3). After Levi has been prepared for office, he is told:

> Levi, thy seed shall be divided into three offices, for a sign of the glory of the Lord who is to come. And the first portion shall be great; yea, greater than it shall none be. The second shall be in the priesthood. And the third shall be called by a new name, because a king shall arise in Judah, and shall establish a new priesthood, after the fashion of the Gentiles (to all the Gentiles). And his presence is beloved, as a prophet of the Most High, of the seed of Abraham our father (8.11 15).

As this pro-Hasmonean propaganda illustrates, supporters of the Maccabean rulers believed that John Hyrcanus combined in his one person the three "anointed" offices; that is, he was a priest who also exercised royal rule and prophetic gifts. However, unlike the biblical models which we have earlier reviewed, there is no hint that Hyrcanus received the charismatic Spirit of prophecy.

The Qumran covenanters quickly became bitter rivals of the Hasmoneans. Opposing the claim that the three "anointed" offices were united in one man, they separated the offices. According to the *Community Rule*, those who sought to join their community "shall be ruled by the primitive precepts in which the men of the Community were first instructed until there shall come the prophet and the Messiahs of Aaron and Israel" (CR IX). The so-called *Messianic Anthology* informs us that this end-time prophet is the eschatological prophet like Moses (Deuteronomy 18:18–19).

Though they still awaited the coming of the eschatological prophet, the Qumran covenanters may have believed that the Holy Spirit (of prophecy) already operated in their midst. In Hymn XII we read:

> I, the Master, know Thee O my God,
>   by the spirit which Thou has given to me,
> and by Thy Holy Spirit I have faithfully hearkened
>   to Thy marvellous counsel.
> In the mystery of Thy wisdom
>   Thou hast opened knowledge to me,

and in Thy mercies
[Thou hast unlocked for me] the fountain of Thy might.

Significantly, in *Jewish Antiquities*, Josephus reports on three Essene prophets: 1) Judas, who foretold the death of Antigonus (XIII. 311–13); 2) Menahem, who foretold that Herod would become "king of the Jews" (XV. 373–8); and 3) Simon, who interpreted a dream of Archelaus to mean that his rule would last ten years (XVII. 345–8). It is tantalizing to speculate that Simon, the Essene prophet, might be identified with the prophet Simeon, who blessed Jesus in the Temple (Luke 2:25–35).

Furthermore, in strongly dualistic terms, the *Community Rule* describes two classes of men who are ruled by "the spirits of truth and falsehood" (CR III–IV). The children of light are ruled by the Angel of Light, who seems to be identified with the Angel of Truth. In contrast, the children of falsehood are ruled by the Angel of Darkness. This terminology of the Spirit, though not the theology, is to be found in the Johannine description of the Spirit-Paraclete (John 14–16).

It is evident that the Qumran covenanters believed that they were the elect community of the last days and, therefore, that some of their leaders, if not the entire community, had received the Holy Spirit. Indeed, some of their Essene brethren were noteworthy prophets. In spite of this claim to have received the Holy Spirit, to be ruled by the Spirit of Truth, and to exercise the prophetic gift, they made little charismatic impact on the destiny of the nation, whom they considered to be apostate.

Rejecting both the Hasmonean and Qumranian messianic-prophetic views, in the turbulent decades which witnessed the transition from Hasmonean to Roman power in Judea, the Pharisees revived the old messianic hope of the restoration of the Davidic Monarchy. This Davidic King would deliver Judah from her oppressors. The author of the *Psalms of Solomon* prays:

Behold, O Lord, and raise up unto them their king, the
  son of David,
  At the time in which thou seest, O God, that he may
  reign over Israel Thy servant.
And gird him with strength, that he may shatter
  unrighteous rulers,
  And that he may purge Jerusalem from nations that
  trample (her) down to destruction (17:23–25).

The psalm also describes the spiritual endowment of this son of David:

> He will bless the people of the Lord with wisdom and
> gladness,
> And he himself (will be) pure from sin, so that he
> may rule a great people.
> He will rebuke rulers, and remove sinners by the might
> of his word;
> And (relying) upon his God, throughout his days he
> will not stumble;
> For God will make him mighty by means of (His) holy
> spirit,
> And wise by means of the spirit of understanding,
> with strength and righteousness (17:40–42).

In language which echoes the gift of the Spirit to both Saul and David (1 Samuel 10:10; 16:13), this son of David will be a charismatic warrior-king.

Apart from these isolated experiences of the restoration of prophetic inspiration in the intertestamental period, the piety of Judaism was identified by its devotion to the Law, rather than charismatic leadership. In fact, devotion to the Law, "by nature, precluded the activity of the Spirit."[7] Thus, interpretation of the Law displaced prophetic inspiration, teaching replaced proclamation, and the scribe replaced the prophet. Because of this preoccupation with Torah piety, in intertestamental Judaism the climate was unfavorable to the restoration of charismatic leadership, generally, and of the restoration of prophetic inspiration, specifically. Thus, the charismatic Spirit of prophecy disappeared from Israel.

It is against this background of the Old Testament record of charismatic leadership, of hope for the coming of an end-time Messiah, one who would be both Spirit-anointed and Spirit-empowered, of hope for a people who would share in the gift of His Spirit, and of the consciousness in Judaism that the prophetic gift of the Spirit was absent, that we must interpret the dramatic and unprecedented outburst of the gift of the Spirit in Luke-Acts.

As we turn to the interpretation of the Holy Spirit in Luke-Acts, we will proceed on the following basis. In general terms, Old Testament and Jewish Hellenistic historiography furnished Luke with the model for writing his two-volume history of the origin and spread of Christianity. Moreover, the charismatic motifs of the Hebrew and Greek Bibles, such as the transfer, sign, and vocational motifs, influence Luke's theology of the Holy Spirit. In addition to the influence of these charismatic motifs, the Septuagint furnishes Luke with the terminology to describe the activity of the Holy Spirit in the lives of Jesus and His disciples. Finally, Luke-Acts contrasts with the intertestamental belief in the cessation of prophetic inspiration; rather, it reports the restoration of prophetic activity after four centuries of silence.

CHAPTER THREE

The Holy Spirit in the Gospel of Luke: The Charismatic Christ

The so-called we passages in Acts[1] are either the memoirs of the writer of Luke-Acts, who is traditionally identified as Luke, or else they are a travel diary formerly kept by one of Paul's companions, perhaps either Silas or Timothy, which an unknown editor subsequently incorporated into his record.[2] If they are the former, and this is the most natural explanation, then Luke, author and sometime companion of Paul, personally participated in the missionary travels of Paul. When he came to write the story of this mission, therefore, Luke was not only able to consult other participants, but he was also able to draw copiously from his own firsthand experience. In order to write the complete history of this mission, however, he had to begin with the origin of this apostolic witness, namely, the gift of the Holy Spirit to the disciples on the day of Pentecost. Moreover, in order to explain Pentecost, he necessarily had to prefix the story of Jesus, the Gospel, to the story of this apostolic witness.

Luke's participation in Paul's mission to the Gentiles partially accounts for the evolution of the gospel genre from Mark's "gospel" to his "history of salvation." When he reduced the story of Jesus to writing, Mark, of necessity, developed this uniquely Christian literature.[3] The Gospel According to Mark is neither history nor biography; according to the tradition of the early church, it is the written record of Peter's preaching in Rome.[4] According to scholarly consensus, Mark's Gospel is the primary source underlying Luke's Gospel. However, by adding the birth narrative, expanding the inauguration narrative, and then setting the whole story into the chronological and geographical framework of Judaism under Imperial Rome, Luke radically altered Mark's "gospel," thereby creating a Christian "history of salvation" as the sequel to the sacred history of Israel.

Furthermore, Luke's participation in Paul's travel, trials, and Roman destination, no doubt, partially shaped the symmetrical structure of Luke-Acts. As the following chart demonstrates, this participation gave Luke the thematic program for forming the story of Jesus and the story of the disciples into two parallel parts.

The Thematic Structure of Luke-Acts

	LUKE	ACTS
Beginning	Birth, anointing of Jesus	Baptism, filling of disciples
Inaugural Proclamation	Jesus' Nazareth sermon	Peter's Pentecost sermon
Confirmatory Miracles	Casting out demons and healing sick in Capernaum	Healing lame man at Beautiful gate
Success	Widespread popular acclaim	Widespread popular acclaim
Opposition	Pharisees, leaders of the Jews	Sanhedrin, Jews of the dispersion
Travel	Itinerant ministry in Galilee, Judea	Missionary journeys of Peter and Paul
Arrest and Trial	Threefold trial: before Sanhedrin, Pilate, and Herod	Threefold trial: before Felix, Festus, and Agrippa
Consummation	The Cross	Rome

This chart is not an outline of the content of Luke-Acts; it simply illustrates that Luke develops both parts of his history of the origin and spread of Christianity around the same thematic structure.

Finally, Luke's participation in the spread of Christianity helps explain the interdependent relationship between the history-of-salvation theme and the charismatic activity of the Holy Spirit. The Gospel is the story of Jesus, the unique charismatic Prophet; the Acts is the story of His disciples, a community of charismatic prophets. As Luke describes it, their respective ministries of salvation are possible only through the

anointing, empowering, and leading of the Holy Spirit. It is this Lukan
emphasis on a charismatic mission which contrasts with the minimal
role of the Spirit in either Mark or Matthew.

In comparison to the other synoptic evangelists, the Holy Spirit is
statistically most numerous in Luke: Mark (6x), Matthew (12x), and
Luke (17x). It is significant that, with some minor exceptions,[5] all of
the references to the Holy Spirit in Mark and Matthew are paralleled in
Luke.[6] Of greater significance is that many references to the Holy Spirit
in Luke are unparalleled in either Mark or Matthew.[7] These texts,
which are concentrated in Luke's infancy and inauguration narratives,
best reflect his unique perspective on the gift of the Spirit. The following diagram illustrates the distribution of references to the Holy Spirit in
the Gospels.

References to the Spirit in the Synoptic Gospels

MARK	MATTHEW	LUKE
1:8	1:18–20*	1:15
1:10	3:11	1:17
1.12	3:16	1:35
3:29	4:1	1:41
12:36	10:20	1:67
13:11	12:18	2:25–27*
	12:28	3:16
	12:31–32*	3:22
	22:43	4:1
	28:19	4:1
		4:14
		10:21
		11:13
		12:10
		12:12

*These texts have multiple references to the Spirit.

This concentration of references to the Holy Spirit in the Gospel of Luke
demonstrates that the Spirit is historically and theologically of more
interest to Luke than it is to the other evangelists. In this chapter we will
investigate Luke's emphasis on the Holy Spirit as it is to be found in the
infancy narrative (1:5-2:52), in the inauguration narrative (3:1-4:44),
and in the individual texts which are scattered throughout the Gospel.

1. The Infancy Narrative (1:5-2:52)

The transition from Luke's prologue (1:1-4) to the infancy narrative plunges the reader into an environment of humble and pietistic Judaism. The narrative focuses upon the righteous and devout (1:6, 28; 2:25) who cluster around the Temple and its worship (1:9; 2:27, 37). As their praise and worship demonstrates, they are steeped in the imagery and thought forms of their Scriptures (1:46-55, 68-79; 2:29-32). Consistent with their devotion, they keep their religious laws and observances (1:59; 2:21-22).

In this atmosphere, strangely pregnant with religious devotion, Luke reports two dramatic birth announcements. First, the angel Gabriel announces to the aged priest, Zacharias, "Your wife Elizabeth will bear you a son, and you will give him the name John" (1:13). Second, some six months later, the same heavenly messenger informs Mary, a young relative of Elizabeth, "You have found favor with God. And behold, you will conceive in your womb, and bear a son, and you shall name Him Jesus" (1:30b-31). Luke's subsequent report of the births of John and Jesus bring these dramatic announcements to their natural conclusion (1:57-2:38).

Equally dramatic, in this atmosphere of piety and cult, an unprecedented outburst of the charismatic activity of the Holy Spirit punctuates these nativity scenes. John, the angel announces, "will be filled with the Holy Spirit, while yet in his mother's womb" (1:15). Moreover, Gabriel informs Mary that she will conceive Jesus in this miraculous manner, "The Holy Spirit will come upon you, and the power of the Most High will overshadow you" (1:35). Furthermore, not only will John be filled with the Holy Spirit, but subsequent events find both his mother, Elizabeth, and his father, Zacharias, "filled with the Holy Spirit" (1:41, 67). Finally, in a remarkable clustering of terms, the aged Simeon has

the Holy Spirit . . . upon him. And it had been revealed to him by the Holy Spirit that he would not see death before he had seen the Lord's Christ. And he came in the Spirit into the Temple (2:25–27).

With the lone exception that Matthew also reports that Mary will conceive Jesus by the overshadowing power of the Holy Spirit (Matthew 1:18–20), Luke's record of this activity of the Spirit in unparalleled in the other Gospels.

As Luke (and Matthew) reports it, the miraculous conception of Jesus by the overshadowing power of the Holy Spirit differs from the other activity of the Spirit in the infancy narrative. It is the creative power of God. In terms which are perhaps reminiscent of the hovering Spirit at creation (Genesis 1:2), in Mary's conception of Jesus the Spirit effects a new creation. This overshadowing of the divine presence signifies that the conception of Jesus has an importance which is similar to the earlier creation of the cosmos. Future events in the life of Jesus will attest to the epochal significance of this unique creative event.

The other four references to the activity of the Holy Spirit in the infancy narrative, in contrast, describe the charismatic activity of the Spirit. Specifically, this charismatic activity is prophetic. For example, John, Elizabeth, and Zacharias are each filled with the Holy Spirit. As the reference to Zacharias makes it explicit (1:67), Luke uses this term to describe prophetic inspiration. Thus, Elizabeth's and Zacharias's songs of praise (1:42–45, 68–79) are prophetic speech. By analogy, because he has the Holy Spirit upon him, Simeon's blessing (2:29–32) is a further example of prophetic inspiration. This charismatic outpouring of the Holy Spirit in the infancy narrative, then, invariably results in prophetic praise and worship.

More important than these outbursts of prophetic praise, the Holy Spirit is given to John for his charismatic mission as the messianic herald (3:1–6). In specific terms, his vocation is prophetic. While yet an unborn child, John is filled with the Holy Spirit for his prophetic vocation (1:15). This gift of the Spirit will enable him to minister in the spirit and power of Elijah (1:17). When John is circumcised, his father Zacharias, inspired by the Spirit, prophesies, "And you, child, will be called the prophet of the Most High" (1:76). Luke, moreover, introduces John's public ministry with a formula which echoes the introductory formulae of many of the Old Testament prophets (3:1–2).

That John should be spoken of in prophetic terms is not surprising. Both his earlier reception of the Spirit and the character of his subsequent ministry are consistent with the prophetic vocation. The people not only recognized him to be a prophet (20:6), however, but stirred by his preaching also wondered "whether he might be the Christ" (3:15). Contemporary Judaism identified the prophetic and messianic vocation. The Qumran literature, for example, witnesses to the widespread popularity of this identification of the prophetic and messianic ministries.[8] This identification of the prophetic and messianic functions in John's ministry is the key to the interpretation of Jesus' Spirit-anointed charismatic ministry.

This dramatic outburst of charismatic or prophetic activity is best interpreted against the background of intertestamental Judaism. In chapter 2 we observed that the extra-canonical literature of this period, though it is characterized by diversity, witnesses to a threefold perspective on the Spirit:[9] 1) in Judaism the Spirit is almost always the Spirit of prophecy, 2) this prophetic gift of the Spirit has ceased with the last of the writing prophets, and 3) the revival of the activity of the Spirit is expected only in the messianic age—however it might be variously conceived.

The infancy narrative reflects a similar perspective. In both the infancy narrative and in Judaism the Spirit is the Spirit of prophecy. Furthermore, they both intimately associate the Spirit with the messianic age. Nevertheless, the activity of the Spirit in the infancy narrative is also in tension with the perspective of Judaism. Whereas Judaism still awaited the messianic restoration of prophetic inspiration, the infancy narrative, in contrast, describes the fulfillment of that intertestamental expectation. Interpreted against the background of Judaism, therefore, the outburst of prophetic inspiration, which Luke reports in the infancy narrative, heralds nothing less than the dawning of the messianic age.

With its episodes of angelic visitations, outbursts of prophecy, and nativity scenes, Luke's infancy narrative contains a variety of typological, programmatic, and paradigmatic elements. For example, in announcing the future birth of John, the angel casts his ministry in the typological pattern of Elijah (1:17). Furthermore, Luke portrays a clear typological correspondence between John and Jesus. John, who is filled with the Holy Spirit, will be a prophet of the Most High (1:15, 76). Similarly, Jesus, who is conceived by the power of the Holy Spirit, will be the Son of the Most High (1:32, 35). Though John is the son of Zacharias and Jesus is the Son of God, the activity of the Holy Spirit, nevertheless, creates a genuine typological correspondence between these two infants, whose births herald the dawning of the messianic age.

In addition to these typological correspondences, the infancy narrative also gives programmatic anticipations of what is to follow. In the first place, as Paul Minear writes in his essay, ''Luke's Use of the Birth Stories'':

There is an observable kinship between the Canticles in the opening chapters, the opening ''keynote addresses'' of John and Jesus (chaps. 3, 4), and the sermons of Acts. . . . Luke's thought gravitates toward and is oriented around strategic speeches, citations, and hymns.[10]

Secondly, these programmatic elements are not limited to strategic speeches, citations, and hymns; they are also to be found in the charismatic activity of the Holy Spirit. In the infancy narrative John, Elizabeth, and Zacharias are filled with the Holy Spirit. This is programmatic for the gift of the Spirit in Acts, beginning with the disciples on the day of Pentecost and ending with the disciples at Iconium (2:4; 13:52). This outburst of charismatic activity is also paradigmatic, for just as it means "prophetic inspiration" in the infancy narrative, it also means "prophetic inspiration" in the Acts.

2. The Inauguration Narrative (3:1–4:44)

Luke launches the public ministry of Jesus by focusing his narrative upon the same two men whose births were so dramatically announced in the infancy narrative—John and Jesus. Just as the birth of John had earlier preceded the birth of Jesus, so now John is at the peak of his popularity as Jesus prepares to inaugurate His own public ministry. In fulfilling his role as herald and in signifying the transition from himself to his successor, John testifies, "As for me, I baptize you with water; but He who is mightier than I is coming, and I am not fit to untie the thong of his sandals; He Himself will baptize you in the Holy Spirit and fire" (3:16).

As the inaugural events unfold, however, He who had been conceived by the overshadowing power of the Holy Spirit and who would baptize in the Holy Spirit must first be anointed by the Holy Spirit (3:22; 4:18). In this way Jesus becomes the Christ, the Anointed One, not only possessing the Spirit, but also subject to the leading of the Spirit and dependent upon the empowering of the Spirit (4:1, 14). Indeed, as Luke portrays the public ministry of Jesus from His baptism until the day of Pentecost, the presence and power of the Spirit is concentrated exclusively upon Him.[11] In Luke's theology, Jesus has become the charismatic Christ—the unique bearer of the Spirit.

In the inauguration narrative, Luke describes the beginning of the public ministry of Jesus in three episodes: 1) His baptism (3:21-22), 2) His temptation (4:1-13), and 3) His inaugural sermon in the synagogue in Nazareth (4:14-30). Though these episodes are both geographically and temporally separated, they form an integrated narrative, the launching of the public ministry of Jesus—the charismatic Christ.

A. The Baptism of Jesus

All four Evangelists record the baptism of Jesus by John the Baptist. Each Evangelist also records the two phenomena which accompanied that baptism: the descent of the Spirit upon Jesus and the voice from heaven. A comparison of the four accounts reveals a fundamental agreement with each other, while at the same time revealing minor differences of detail. These differences are significant for they reflect the unique perspective of each Evangelist. For example, for both Luke and Mark, "The act of baptism is subordinated to the subsequent imparting of the Holy Spirit."[12] In contrast, by emphasizing the dialogue between John and Jesus concerning the appropriateness of Jesus being baptized, Matthew gives greater emphasis to the act of baptism.

Further differences exist between the Evangelists. Matthew, Mark, and John all report that the Holy Spirit descended "like a dove" (Matthew 3:16, Mark 1:10, John 1:32), whereas Luke reports that the Spirit descended "in bodily form like a dove" (Luke 3:22). By this qualification Luke emphasizes that the descent of the Spirit upon Jesus was not a mystical or visionary experience. It was, rather, an objective, externalized, and physical manifestation of the Spirit.

Concomitant with the descent of the Holy Spirit, a voice from heaven declares, "Thou art My beloved Son, in Thee I am well pleased" (3:22). This heavenly voice at Jesus' baptism is analogous to the "voice" (phonē) in Josephus (Ant XIII X.3) or to the "echo" of His voice (bat kol) in rabbinic literature. It was commonly believed in Judaism that with the death of the last prophets God communicated His will only occasionally, and then only by a heavenly voice (Tos Sot 13, 2). Both the descent of the Holy Spirit and the voice from heaven at Jesus' baptism attest that with Jesus God is restoring the broken communication between himself and Israel.

The heavenly declaration, "Thou art my beloved Son, in Thee I am well pleased," directs us to the Old Testament. This declaration echoes two texts, Psalm 2:7 (Thou art my Son), and Isaiah 42:1 (in whom My soul delights). Interpreters commonly believe that this designated Jesus to be both the Davidic king of the psalm and the servant of Isaiah.[13] This interpretation is, however, open to question. The immediate context of the temptation (4:1ff) and the hostility (4:28ff) which Jesus would soon experience weakens this interpretation. In the light of this context the voice from heaven encourages and strengthens Jesus for the satanic and human opposition He must face.

A similar voice from heaven some time later confirms this alternative interpretation. It, too, is in the context of impending opposition. Jesus has just warned His disciples that "The Son of Man must suffer many things, and be rejected by the elders and chief priests and scribes, and be killed, and be raised upon the third day" (9:22). Conscious of this fate which awaits Him, Jesus goes up to the mountain to pray. While He prays a voice comes out of a cloud saying, "This is my Son, My Chosen One; listen to Him!" (9:35). The voice from heaven encourages and strengthens Jesus, as at His baptism, in anticipation of the hostility which culminates in his death.

The Second Psalm has a similar message for the Davidic king as the heavenly voice has for Jesus. God assures the Davidic king that, though enemies and opposition may encircle him, nevertheless, he enjoys divine favor and protection. In terms which anticipate the filial relationship between Jesus and the Father, the psalm assures the king that God acts toward him in the manner of a father toward his son.

In conclusion, the voice from heaven does not designate Jesus to be the Davidic king. Rather, it expresses the Father's commendation to His Son engaged in the battle against the hostile forces of evil. Encouraged and strengthened by this divine commendation, Jesus will press the battle to its victorious climax.

B. The Temptation of Jesus (4:1-13)

Each of the synoptic Evangelists connects the temptation of Jesus with His reception of the Spirit. After His baptism the Spirit leads (Matthew 4:1, Luke 4:1) or impells (Mark 1:12) Jesus to go into the wilderness for a period of testing by Satan. Luke alone qualifies Jesus as "full of the Holy Spirit" (4:1). In his commentary on the Gospel of Luke, Alfred Plummer observes:

Jesus had been endowed with supernatural power; and He was tempted to make use of it in furthering His own interests without regard to the Father's will. . . . He went into the desert in obedience to the Spirit's promptings. That He should be *tempted* there was the Divine purpose respecting Him, to prepare Him for his work.[14]

Thus the gift of the Spirit to Jesus not only occasions the temptation, but also gives meaning to the temptation.

Luke is also alone in recording the fact that following this period of temptation, "Jesus returned to Galilee in the power of the Spirit; and news about Him spread through all the surrounding district" (4:14). Both Matthew and Mark associate the commencement of Jesus' Galilean ministry with the imprisonment of John the Baptist (Matthew 4:12, Mark 1:14). By his silence about John's imprisonment Luke emphasizes Jesus' pneumatic or charismatic empowering.

C. The Preaching of Jesus in Nazareth (4:14-30)

Though all four Evangelists record the descent of the Spirit upon Jesus after His baptism by John, Luke alone records Jesus' understanding of that event. Participating in the synagogue service one sabbath after His return to Galilee, Jesus reads from the prophet Isaiah:

The Spirit of the Lord is upon Me,
Because He anointed Me to preach the gospel to the poor,
He has sent Me to proclaim release to the captives,
And recovery of sight to the blind,
To set free those who are downtrodden,
To proclaim the favorable year of the Lord (4:18–19).

Returning the scroll to the attendant, He announces to the congregation, "Today this Scripture has been fulfilled in your hearing" (4:21). Jesus thus understands that the descent of the Spirit upon Him at His baptism effected His anointing. Hence Jesus is the "Anointed One," the "Messiah" (Hebrew), or the "Christ" (Greek), longed for by the devout Simeon (2:26) and scores of his contemporaries, whether from pietistic or nationalistic motives.

Many in Israel were the Lord's anointed. Priests (Exodus 28:41), kings (1 Samuel 10:1), and even prophets (1Kings 19:16) were anointed to office. Moreover, even a foreign monarch like Cyrus could be called the Lord's anointed (Isaiah 45:1). The problem which confronts the interpreter of Luke is: to which of these offices was Jesus anointed by the descent of the Spirit? Although interpreters often deny that Jesus either claimed to be or thought of himself as a prophet,[15] the Lukan data lead to the conclusion that Jesus claimed to fulfill the prophetic ministry.

Significantly, Judaism understood Isaiah 61:1 in prophetic terms. The Targum of Jonathan renders the Hebrew text of Isaiah 61:1 in Aramaic as, "The Spirit of prophecy from before the Lord God is upon me."[16] Now, in a synagogue service:

After the Prayer (Tephillah) came the reading of the Scriptures, accompanied in Palestine by a rendering into Aramaic. Then came the homily which in Palestine was for the greater part in Aramaic.[17]

Luke's description of this synagogue service at Nazareth, "corresponds exactly to what the Mishnah and later Jewish texts have on synagogue usage."[18] Thus, it is highly probable that the Aramaic rendering, "The Spirit of prophecy," was part of the Nazareth service. The Aramaic character of the text would have disappeared when Luke (or his source) assimilated the text to the Greek Septuagint translation of Isaiah.

The reaction of the crowd to Jesus' homily indicates that He claimed to be a prophet. Luke reports that "all were speaking well of Him, and wondering at the gracious words which were falling from His lips; and they were saying, 'Is this not Joseph's son?' " (4:22). In response, Jesus challenges them to accept Him, not as Joseph's son, but as a prophet. He chides the crowd, "Truly I say to you, no prophet is welcome in his home town" (4:24). It is unlikely that Jesus is simply appealing to a proverbial saying which illustrates His imminent rejection. Rather, in the light of Isaiah 61:1, especially its Targumic rendering, Jesus claims to be the anointed servant/prophet. Recognizing His claim, yet rejecting it, the crowd attempts to kill Him (4:28-30).

Conscious that the descent of the Holy Spirit anointed Him for a charismatic ministry, Jesus deliberately models His public ministry after three Old Testament prophets: Isaiah, Elijah, and Moses.[19] In the prophet Isaiah Jesus found the model for His anointed ministry of consolation and teaching. The heavenly voice at His baptism bestowed upon Him the ministry of the prophet-servant, of whom God declares, "I have put My Spirit upon him" (Isaiah 42:1). Similarly, the anointing of the Spirit gave Him the evangel—His ministry of good news to the afflicted, brokenhearted, captives, and prisoners (Isaiah 61:1). Finally, in His parabolic teaching, He deliberately parallels the mission of Isaiah to Judah (Luke 8:9-10; Isaiah 6:10).

Jesus also patterns His prophetic ministry after the charismatic prophets, Elijah and Elisha. In the city of Nain Jesus raises a widow's son from the dead, and the people exclaim, "A great prophet has arisen among us" (7:16). This, and many other miracles, earned Jesus the widespread reputation of a great prophet. His reputation greatly perplexed Herod the tetrarch, John's murderer, for "it was said by some that John has risen from the dead, and by some that Elijah had appeared, and by others, that one of the prophets of old had risen again" (9:7b-8). Similarly, the disciples report that among the common people Jesus is reputed to be John, Elijah, or one of the other prophets come to life (9:19). This reputation was justified, for as the following chart illustrates, Jesus' public ministry parallels that of the charismatic prophets, Elijah and Elisha.

Parallels Between Elijah, Elisha, and Jesus

	ELIJAH	ELISHA	JESUS
Control Nature	1 Kings 17:1 2 Kings 2:8	2 Kings 2:14 2 Kings 2:19ff	Luke 8:22ff
Raise the dead	1 Kings 17:17ff	2 Kings 4:34f	Luke 7:14f
Multiply food	1 Kings 17:16	2 Kings 4:3ff 2 Kings 4:42ff	Luke 9:12ff
Heal leprosy		2 Kings 5:8ff	Luke 5:12f

Jesus' ministry parallels that of Elijah and Elisha in at least three other respects. First, like Elijah and Elisha, Jesus is empowered by the Spirit (2 Kings 2:9, 14-15, Luke 4:14). Second, like Elijah and Elisha, He will be rejected and minister to strangers (4:24-30). Finally, just as there was a transfer of the Spirit from Elijah to Elisha, so there will be a transfer of the Spirit from Jesus to His disciples (Acts 2:4, 33). These parallels have a twofold significance: 1) they confirm that the public ministry of Jesus is charismatic and prophetic, and 2) they demonstrate that Jesus is the eschatological Elijah; that is, the last days have arrived in Him. As Peter recognizes, this can only mean that Jesus is the Christ (9:20).

Finally, Jesus is also the prophet like Moses described in Deuteronomy 18:15, "The Lord your God will raise up for you a prophet like me from among you, from your countrymen, you shall listen to Him." This phrase, "you shall listen to Him" is echoed in the transfiguration account. In response to Peter's suggestion that they build three tabernacles: one each for Moses, Elijah, and Jesus, a voice comes out of the cloud, saying, "This is my Son, My Chosen One; listen to Him!" (9:35). Very likely it is Peter's experience here on the Mount of Transfiguration which later causes him to identify Jesus as the Prophet like Moses (Acts 3:22). This apparently became a widespread identification in the early Church, for even the Hellenistic Jew, Stephen, makes this identification (Acts 7:37).

All three prophets were endowed with the Spirit; that is, they were charismatic leaders. Moreover, in contemporary Judaism both Moses and Elijah were end-time or messianic figures. And so, both singly and collectively, they formed an appropriate model for the charismatic or Spirit-anointed ministry of Jesus.

We have observed that the presence and activity of the Holy Spirit dominates Luke's inauguration narrative. Only from Luke do we learn that Jesus begins His ministry "anointed" by the Spirit. Luke alone observes that Jesus, when tested in the wilderness, is full of the Spirit. Only Luke records that Jesus begins His Galilean ministry in the power of the Spirit. The other Evangelists all fail to parallel this activity of the Spirit, which for Luke prefaces the public ministry of Jesus.

The gift of the Spirit to Jesus in the inauguration narrative, like the gift of the Spirit to John in the infancy narrative, is vocational. This vocational gift is specifically prophetic. Jesus is not only anointed by the Spirit, but He is also Spirit-led, Spirit-filled, and Spirit-empowered. The outburst of prophetic activity associated with the birth announcements of John and Jesus heralds the dawning of the messianic age. The activity of the Spirit in the baptism, temptation, and synagogue episodes inaugurates the public ministry of Jesus the Messiah. For Luke, Jesus ministers as the eschatological charismatic prophet.

The typological, programmatic, and paradigmatic elements which are found in the infancy narrative are also to be found in the episodes which collectively constitute the inauguration narrative. Paradoxically, just as Elijah is a type for the prophetic ministry of John the Baptist (1:17), so he is also a type for the prophetic ministry of Jesus (4:26). Similarly, both Isaiah and Moses typify some aspects of the prophetic ministry of Jesus.

In addition, Luke intends the Spirit's anointing, leading, and empowering of Jesus to be programmatic for His entire ministry. His programmatic description of the Spirit in the inauguration narrative echoes the programmatic character of the gift of the Spirit to both Moses and Elijah (Numbers 11:16ff, 2 Kings 2:1ff). In other words, just as a single, almost incidental reference to the Spirit in the lives of these two leaders points to a widespread charismatic ministry, so Luke's references to the Spirit in the inauguration narrative signify that from His baptism to His ascension the *entire* ministry of Jesus is charismatic.

Luke also invests a paradigmatic significance to the gift of the Spirit in the inauguration narrative. That is, just as the ministry of Jesus, as the Christ, must be charismatic and inaugurated by the anointing of the Spirit, so the ministry of His disciples, heirs and successors to His own ministry, must be both charismatic (Acts 1:8), and inaugurated by the baptizing-filling of the Spirit (Acts 1:5; 2:4). In the ongoing history of salvation, at Pentecost the ministry of the charismatic Christ is transferred to a *necessarily charismatic* community of disciples.

3. Individual Texts

It remains for us to survey the four remaining references to the Holy Spirit in the Gospel of Luke (10:21; 11:13; 12:10; 12:12). These texts, either singly or collectively, lack the importance of the infancy and inauguration narratives for understanding Luke's theology of the Holy Spirit. Though they make no significant contribution to Luke's theology, nevertheless, they highlight the importance of the Holy Spirit in Lukan thought.

Both Luke and Matthew incorporate a common source, commonly designated *Q*, into their respective Gospels. Two *Q*-texts reflect the importance of the Holy Spirit for Luke: Jesus' thanksgiving to the Father (Luke 10:21-22; Matthew 11:25-27), and Jesus' encouragement to pray (Luke 11:9-13, Matthew 7:7-11). In the first text, in comparison with Matthew, Luke adds the qualification that Jesus, "rejoiced greatly in the Holy Spirit" (10:21). In the second text Luke substitutes "Holy Spirit" for Matthew's "good things" (11:13).

How do we account for these differences? While Matthew has undoubtedly preserved the original wording, Luke has altered his source. This fact does not threaten Luke's reliability, for his modifications conform to the common principle of midrash pesher; that is, contemporizing the text, "fitting it to its 'fulfillment' in the writer's own time."[20] Because of his emphasis on the Holy Spirit, Luke contemporizes the original promise of "good things" to the post-Pentecost reality of the gift of the Spirit. While the meaning is consistent with the *Q*-source, the wording is Luke's.

In common with Matthew, Luke is dependent upon Mark for the two remaining references to the Holy Spirit: the saying about blasphemy against the Holy Spirit (Luke 12:10, Mark 3:29, Matthew 12:31), and Jesus' promise of the Holy Spirit's teaching (Luke 12:12, Mark 13:11, Matthew 10:20). Minor stylistic variations characterize the three accounts. For example, both Mark and Luke have "Holy Spirit," whereas Matthew has "Spirit" and "Spirit of your Father." In spite of these variations, the three accounts reflect a similar theological perspective.

What do these four texts contribute to Luke's theology of the Holy Spirit? Two texts—Jesus' rejoicing in the Spirit (10:21), and his promise of the Spirit's teaching (12:12)—reinforce Luke's earlier emphasis on the Holy Spirit as the source of inspiration. We also learn that the disciples can petition the Father for the gift of the Spirit. This perspective is unique to Luke and no doubt reflects the post-Pentecost reality of the gift of the Spirit. Perhaps Luke understood the case of Ananias and Sapphira to be one example of the sin against the Holy Spirit. We cannot say for certain. At the least, the saying about blasphemy against the Spirit cautions against attributing the works of God to the power of Satan.

As Herod's reign draws to its tragic and turbulent end, two angelic birth announcements occasion an outburst of prophetic activity. Before a generation passes the prophetic voice is again heard in Israel, exhorting the people to repent and be baptized, for God's reign is imminent. The people wonder: Is this prophet Elijah, or is he the Christ? However, soon a carpenter's son from Galilee fires the popular imagination. He claims to be anointed by the Spirit, a claim which his miracles authenticate. Suddenly, after generations of silence, the presence and power of the Spirit are manifested in Israel, signifying that the messianic age has dawned.

Among the Evangelists, Luke gives the greatest emphasis to this renewal of charismatic or prophetic activity. He did so, no doubt, because he believed that it made a vital contribution toward illuminating the meaning of the gift of the Spirit, not only to the disciples on the day of Pentecost but also to the Samaritans, Saul, the household of Cornelius, and the disciples at Ephesus. For Luke it is impossible to divorce either the mission of Jesus from the activity of the Spirit, or the mission of the disciples from the activity of the Spirit.

One startling fact, however, emerges from the study of the Holy Spirit in the Gospel of Luke: Jesus rarely mentions the Holy Spirit in His teaching. This silence is bound up with Jesus' reluctance to openly declare his Messiahship. C.K. Barrett writes:

Jesus was the Messiah; *as such* he was the bearer of the Spirit. But he kept his Messiahship secret . . . Jesus himself hardly ever spoke of the Spirit; he could not have done so . . . without declaring the Messiahship which it was his purpose to keep secret.[21]

Though Barrett's observation is correct, it must not lead us to the wrong conclusion, namely, that the Holy Spirit is unimportant for the Gospel story.

Rather than the teaching of Jesus about the Holy Spirit, it is the charismatic activity of the Spirit which dominates Luke's account. The presence and power of the Spirit effects the restoration of prophecy and the conception and the anointing of Jesus. Moreover, the leading, fullness, and power of the Spirit characterize the inauguration of His messianic ministry. Thus, in the charismatic theology of St. Luke, the Holy Spirit plays a leading role on the stage of salvation history.

CHAPTER FOUR

The Holy Spirit at Pentecost: The Charismatic Community

In the structure of Luke-Acts, the Pentecost narrative stands in the same relationship to the Acts as the infancy-inauguration narratives do to the Gospel. In the Gospel of Luke these narratives not only introduce the motifs which define the mission of Jesus, but they also show that Jesus will execute His mission in the power of the Holy Spirit. In a similar manner, the Pentecost narrative introduces both the future mission of the disciples and the complementary empowering of the Spirit.

The Pentecost narrative is the story of the transfer of the charismatic Spirit from Jesus to the disciples. In other words, having become the exclusive bearer of the Holy Spirit at His baptism, Jesus becomes the giver of the Spirit at Pentecost. Peter explains the Pentecostal gift of the Spirit, announcing:

Therefore having been exalted to the right hand of God, and having received from the Father the promise of the Holy Spirit, He [Jesus] has poured forth this which you both see and hear (Acts 2:33).

By this transfer of the Spirit, the disciples become the heirs and successors to the earthly charismatic ministry of Jesus; that is, because Jesus has poured out the charismatic Spirit upon them the disciples will continue to do and teach those things which Jesus began to do and teach (Acts 1:1).

This inaugural gift of the Holy Spirit on the day of Pentecost is a pivotal event in Luke's history-of-salvation theology. Therefore, it is not surprising to observe that Luke gives a multiplex description to this transfer of the Spirit. Because of the charismatic-prophetic dimension of Pentecost, Luke's favorite phrase, "filled with the Holy Spirit," best approximates the full meaning of the gift of the Spirit. No single term, however, is sufficiently comprehensive to adequately convey the full meaning of this event. Therefore, in Luke's narrative it is at once a clothing, a baptizing, an empowering, a filling, and an outpouring of the Spirit. As Luke uses these terms, they are essentially synonymous. Each term, however, also contributes distinctive and important nuances to the meaning of this complex phenomenon.

Luke also describes the gift of the Spirit from a fourfold perspective: 1) promise, 2) description, 3) interpretation, and 4) application. First, he records three promises of the Spirit which are fulfilled on the day of Pentecost (Luke 24:49, Acts 1:5, 8). Next, Luke describes the signs which attest to the reality of the outpouring of the Spirit (Acts 2:1–4). He then records Peter's interpretation of the gift of the Spirit (Acts 2:14–21). Finally, he records Peter's application of the pentecostal reality to his audience (Acts 2:37–39). Following an exposition of these data, we will also investigate the possible influence of the Sinai tradition upon Luke's narrative, and the meaning of the religious experience of receiving the Spirit.

1. The Promise of Pentecost (Luke 24:49; Acts 1:5, 8)

A. Clothed with Power

Prior to His ascension Jesus instructed His disciples to wait in Jerusalem until they had received what His Father had promised. This was a promise that the disciples would be "clothed with power from on high" (Luke 24:49).

This word "clothed" normally describes the putting on or wearing of garments. John the Baptist, for example, wore clothing made of camel's hair (Mark 1:6). The father of the returned prodigal son commanded, "Quickly bring out the best robe and put it on him" (Luke 15:22). When mocking Jesus after His trial the soldiers "dressed Him up in purple" (Mark 15:17). This was similar to the robe worn by Herod as he sat on his throne and addressed the crowd at Caesarea (Acts 12:21). The promise that the disciples would be clothed with power is a metaphor analogous to this usage: just as men are clothed with garments, so the disciples will be clothed with power.

In the Septuagint we find a remarkable correspondence between the terminology used by Jesus and several descriptions of the activity of the Spirit of God. Gideon (Judges 6:34), Amasai (1 Chronicles 12:18), and Zechariah the son of Jehoiada (2 Chronicles 24:20) are clothed with, respectively, the Spirit of the Lord, the Spirit, and the Spirit of God. Of course, these terms are synonymous in their contexts and would have been equated with the Holy Spirit by the disciples.

This promise is consistent with the commissioning of the Twelve by Jesus (Luke 9:1–6). Having called the Twelve together, Jesus "gave them power and authority over all the demons, and to heal diseases" (Luke 9:1). Through the exercise of this power the disciples became partners with Jesus in manifesting the kingdom of God—liberating captives from their bondage to the spirit world and restoring many others to health. The disciples, undoubtedly, would have understood this latter promise in the light of their earlier commissioning.

They would also have associated this promise of power with that display of power which had characterized the ministry of Jesus (Luke 4:14). It was a power which could be described in almost physical terms, as when Luke records, "And all the multitude were trying to touch Him, for power was coming from Him and healing *them* all" (Luke 6:19, cf 8:46). The earlier gift of power (Luke 9:1ff), and the post-resurrection reiteration of this gift, can only mean that the disciples, as it were apprentices, are equipped for continuing the ministry which Jesus had inaugurated.

B. Baptized with the Spirit

John the Baptist contrasted his ministry with that of the coming Messiah, "As for me, I baptize you with water; . . . He Himself will baptize you in the Holy Spirit and fire" (Luke 3:16). John's harvest metaphor suggests that this will be both a baptism of blessing, "[He will] gather the wheat into His barn," and of judgment, "He will burn up the chaff with unquenchable fire" (Luke 3:17). As the ministry of Jesus unfolds, however, judgment precedes blessing. Echoing John's warning, Jesus says, "I have come to cast fire upon the earth; and how I wish it were already kindled! But I have a baptism to undergo; and how distressed I am until it is accomplished" (Luke 12:49–50). Anticipating His imminent ascension, Jesus promises the Spirit to the disciples as a blessing, "You shall be baptized with the Holy Spirit not many days from now" (Acts 1:5).

Luke parallels the Spirit baptism of the disciples with the inaugural anointing of Jesus by the Holy Spirit. In his book, *Literary Patterns, Theological Themes and the Genre of Luke-Acts*, Charles Talbert outlines Luke's fourfold parallelism between the two episodes: 1) both Jesus and the disciples are praying, 2) the Spirit descends after their prayers, 3) there is a physical manifestation of the Spirit, and 4) the ministries of both Jesus and the disciples begin with a sermon which is thematic of what follows, appeals to the fulfillment of prophecy, and speaks of the rejection of Jesus.[1] This parallelism points to the functional equivalence between the two events. Therefore, since the gift of the Spirit to Jesus inaugurates and empowers His mission, then, whatever meaning Spirit baptism might have in other contexts, it has the same primary charismatic meaning for the mission of the disciples as the anointing by the Spirit had for the charismatic mission of Jesus.[2]

C. Empowered by the Spirit

The outpouring of the Spirit upon the disciples on the day of Pentecost fulfills the promise of power for mission (Acts 1:8). This latter promise of power differs from the earlier promise (Luke 24:49) in that it is more specific. This power is not some impersonal force but is, in fact, a manifestation of the Spirit. This promise also reveals the purpose of the gift of the Spirit: it is for witness. The particular content of this witness is to be the disciples' attestation to the resurrection of Jesus (Acts 1:22), which, beginning with Peter's Pentecost address, characterizes the preaching of Acts. The gift of the Spirit is thus an equipping of the disciples for service.

In this final promise Jesus describes the Holy Spirit as "coming upon" the disciples. This terminology reflects typical Old Testament descriptions of the coming of the Spirit, for example, upon Balaam (Numbers 24:2), Othniel (Judges 3:10), and Jephthah (Judges 11:29). The example of Samson is of particular significance because of its close association of power with the reception of the Spirit. Several times we read of Samson that "the Spirit of the Lord came upon him mightily" (Judges 14:6; 14:19; 15:14).

This close association between the gift of the Spirit and power, as we have seen, also characterizes the Gospel period. It is true for Mary's conception of Jesus (Luke 1:35), John the Baptist (Luke 1:17), and, most importantly, for Jesus (Luke 4:14). The promise of power as a manifestation of the Spirit assures the disciples that Jesus will not abandon them to their own resources. Rather, they will be fully equipped for their task as witnesses. Indeed, they will receive the same power by which Jesus executed His earthly ministry. Therefore, just as the mission of Jesus had been inaugurated in the power of the Spirit, so at Pentecost the mission of the disciples will be inaugurated in the power of the Spirit.

2. The Miracle of Pentecost (2:1–4)

On the first post-Easter day of Pentecost, the Holy Spirit is poured out upon the waiting disciples with sudden and dramatic impact. The thronging Pentecostal pilgrims hear, but do not feel the force of a violent wind; they see tongues of fire which do not consume, and they hear a group of Galilean provincials ecstatically worshipping God. Each pilgrim hears these Galileans—and this is what creates the sensation—praising God in the language which is native to his homeland.[3] What can this mean?

Luke attributes the unusual behavior of the disciples on the day of Pentecost to their being "filled with the Holy Spirit" (Acts 2:4); others, of course, attribute their exuberance to drunkenness (Acts 2:13). With but one exception (Ephesians 5:18) the phrase "filled with the Holy Spirit" is unique to the Lukan writings. Not only is this term peculiarly Lukan, but it is also his most common description for the activity of the Holy Spirit.

Luke uses the phrase "filled with the Holy Spirit" nine times in Luke-Acts. The following table illustrates his usage of this term.

TEXT	PERSONS	NO	TENSE	PHENOMENON
Lk 1:15	John	1	fut pass	prophetic ministry
Lk 1:41	Elizabeth	1	aor pass	prophecy
Lk 1:67	Zacharias	1	aor pass	prophecy
Ac 2:4	Disciples	Gr	aor pass	glossolalia/prophecy
Ac 4:8	Peter	1	aor pass	witness
Ac 4:31	Disciples	Gr	aor pass	witness
Ac 9:17	Paul	1	aor pass subj	none recorded
Ac 13:9	Paul	1	aor pass	judgment pronounced
Ac 13:52	Disciples	Gr	imperf pass	joy

These data yield several observations. First, the gift of the Spirit to the disciples on the day of Pentecost is not an isolated and unique event. It is but one of several occasions, both prior to and following Pentecost, when people are filled with the Spirit. The experience is the same whether it is Zacharias or Peter who is filled with the Spirit.[4]

Second, being filled with the Spirit is both an individual and a collective phenomenon. Five individuals, John, Elizabeth, Zacharias,

Peter, and Paul, are "filled" on specific occasions. The Jerusalem (2x) and the Iconium disciples experience group fillings. It is important to observe that individuals, Peter and Paul, experience this filling after Pentecost; thus, the post-Pentecost fillings are not solely a collective, a church, experience.

Third, being filled with the Spirit is not a once-for-all experience. The examples of Peter (Acts 2:4; 4:8; 4:31) and Paul (Acts 9:17; 13:9) demonstrate the potentially repetitive character of the gift. Basing his argument on the temporal relationship between a participle and its verb, Howard M. Ervin challenges this interpretation.[5] Since the aorist participle usually describes an action which precedes the main verb, he concludes that Luke's descriptions of Peter (Acts 4:8) and Paul (Acts 13:9) point to their previous filling by the Spirit (Acts 2:4; 9:17). However, when the main verb—in this case "said"—is in the past tense, then the aorist participle describes an action which is contemporaneous with, and not prior to, the main verb.[6] For these examples of Peter and Paul, then, filled with the Spirit describes a repetitive phenomenon.

Luke's use of the aorist indicative for seven of the nine references confirms the potentially repetitive character of being filled with the Spirit. Here the aorist tense simply carries its normative function or punctilliar action; action described "simply as an event, neither on the one hand picturing it in progress, nor on the other affirming the existence of its result."[7] This contrasts with the ingressive aorist which would give the meaning "became filled with the Holy Spirit." If Luke's aorists are ingressive aorists, then on the day of Pentecost the disciples would have entered into the permanent and continuous state of being filled with the Spirit. Obviously this did not happen.

Fourth, filled with the Spirit always describes inspiration. To be filled with the Spirit invariably results in one of several speech patterns. The Iconium disciples being "filled with joy and with the Holy Spirit" (Acts 13:52) is only an apparent exception, for in Luke's perspective joy is as much a matter of inspiration as is prophecy (Luke 10:21). Twice Luke identifies the speech pattern which results from being filled with the Spirit. First, Zacharias is filled with the Holy Spirit and prophesies (Luke 1:67), and second, Peter identifies tongues-speaking with prophecy (Acts 2:4; 2:17). Guided by these identifications, we can also identify the other speech patterns as prophetic. Clearly, for example, Elizabeth's song of praise (Luke 1:42–45) has the same prophetic character as does the prophecy of Zacharias. It seems to be an inescapable

Isaiah and Ezekiel, who announce the inward renewal of the Spirit, but rather appeals to Joel, who announces the restoration of the prophetic activity of the Spirit. Peter's use of Joel, on the one hand, and Luke's parallel between the anointing of Jesus and the Spirit baptism of the disciples, on the other hand, make it clear that Pentecost stands in continuity with the charismatic activity of the Spirit in Old Testament times and in the ministry of Jesus.

4. Peter's Pentecost Application (2:37–39)

Peter's sermon convicts many of the Pentecost pilgrims, and they ask, "Brethren, what shall we do?" (Acts 2:37). Peter replies:

Repent, and let each of you be baptized in the name of Jesus Christ for the forgiveness of your sins; and you shall receive the gift of the Holy Spirit. For the promise is for you and your children, and for all who are afar off, as many as the Lord our God shall call to Himself (Acts 2:38–39).

Peter's application of his message to his audience has a threefold emphasis.

First, Peter points his enquirers to the way of salvation. In words which echo the earlier offer of the gospel by both John the Baptist and Jesus (Mark 1:4, 15), Peter commands, "Repent . . . and be baptized," (Acts 2:38); that is, "Be saved from this perverse generation!" (Acts 2:40). In other words, just as both John and Jesus had radically rejected the racial presumption of the Jews in regards to their salvation, so Peter, the prophet of Pentecost, also challenges these devout pilgrims to abandon their spiritual complacency and receive God's forgiveness.

Second, Peter restricts the eschatological gift of the Spirit to the penitent, the saved. As he addressed the crowd Peter had announced that the last days had arrived—both the Christ and the Spirit were operative in Israel. Undoubtedly, this announcement aroused a false expectation among the pilgrims, namely, that they would also freely participate in the promised eschatological gift of the Spirit which they had just witnessed. Having first denied their automatic participation in salvation, Peter now denies their automatic reception of the Spirit. While Joel announced the eschatological gift of prophecy for "all mankind," Peter informs his audience that the term means "all the penitent," not "all Israel."

Third, Peter announces that the prophetic gift of the Spirit is potentially universal. Its universality includes the temporal dimension—from generation to generation (Acts 2:39). Furthermore, in the language of

Joel, its universality extends to the social dimension: to the young as well as to the old, to female as well as to male, and to slaves as well as to freemen (Acts 2:17–18). Finally, Jesus had earlier promised that the empowering of the Spirit would be geographically limitless—from Jerusalem to Judea to Samaria to the remotest part of the earth (Acts 1:8). In Peter's perspective, then, the eschatological prophethood of all believers extends to all the penitent in every generation, wherever they might live.

5. Pentecost and the Mosaic Tradition

Interpreters often suggest that the Pentecost narrative reflects the conceptual milieu of certain Mosaic traditions. More particularly, they believe that the narrative shares the perspective with certain rabbinic traditions which equate the feast of Pentecost with the giving of the law at Sinai. As R. Eleazer said, "Pentecost [is] the day on which the Law was given" (Peshahim 68b).[8] This rabbinic tradition developed to include the belief that when the law was promulgated, it was heard not only by Israel, but that it was also heard by the seventy-two nations of the world in their own languages. Thus, the Pentecostal tongues of fire, the tongues-speaking, and the catalogue of nations, when interpreted against this tradition represent a "Christianized" Sinai. This rabbinic tradition, however, is demonstrably later than the Pentecost narrative and, therefore, cannot have influenced Luke's description of the gift of the Spirit.[9] In fact, it is probable that the rabbinic tradition developed to oppose the claims of the early Church to having received the gift of the Spirit on the day of Pentecost.[10]

Rather than reflecting contemporary rabbinic traditions, the phenomena of Pentecost—the wind, fire, and the prophecy of the disciples—reflect an Old Testament heritage. The wind and fire are reminiscent of the Exodus narrative. We read that the Lord led the nation out of Egypt, "going before them in a pillar of . . . fire by night" (Exodus 13:21). Furthermore, the Lord delivered the Israelites from the pursuing Egyptian armies when He "swept the sea *back* by a strong east wind all night" (Exodus 14:21). The wind and fire on the day of Pentecost do not, however, attest to a new exodus. Rather, in concrete terms familiar to all, they demonstrate that God was present and active.

In the transfer of the Spirit from Moses to the seventy elders (Numbers 11:10–30) we encounter an event which is in many ways analogous to Pentecost. A brief summary of the two events enables us to better understand the Pentecost event. Inaugurating a new era in Israel's leadership, God permits Moses to share his responsibilities with seventy elders of the nation. Confirming the elders for leadership, God takes the Spirit off of Moses and gives it to the elders. As a result of receiving the Spirit the elders prophesy. The gift of the Spirit at Pentecost reflects the same essential features. For the disciples the ascension marks the end of their apprenticeship and the beginning of their missionary task for which their discipleship had prepared them. Confirming and equipping them for their new responsibilities, Jesus gives the Spirit to them (Acts 2:33). As a result of receiving the Spirit the disciples prophesy.

Both narratives record the transfer of leadership from a single individual to a group. Concomitant with this shift of responsibility, the Spirit is also transferred and placed upon the group. In both cases the transfer of the Spirit results in an outburst of prophecy. When Joshua suggests that Eldad and Medad, who are reported to be prophesying in the camp, be forbidden to prophesy, Moses expresses the earnest desire, "Would that all the Lord's people were prophets, that the Lord would put His Spirit upon them!" (Numbers 11:29). The gift of the Spirit to the disciples on the day of Pentecost, as seen through the eyes of the prophet Joel, fulfills Moses' earnest desire. With the outpouring of the Holy Spirit upon the disciples, the age of the prophethood of all believers has dawned.

6. The Religious Experience of Pentecost

Picture the disciples following the arrest, trial, and crucifixion of Jesus. They had abandoned themselves to the person and ministry of Jesus, but in His death they had experienced a betrayal of their commitment, their hopes, and their aspirations. Shattered, disillusioned, and afraid of possible action against them by the Sanhedrin, they had drifted back to their former occupations. Yet less than two months later, Peter, who had so recently denied any association with Jesus, proclaims before a crowd of thousands that Jesus is the Messiah. A short time later the Council arrests Peter and John and brings them to trial. Characterized by boldness and confidence, Peter testifies to the belief that salvation can only be found in Jesus—the One whom this same Council had so recently condemned to death. What is the explanation for this dramatic change in the disciples?

The resurrection, so apologists answer, accounts for the new dynamism of the disciples. Writing of the resurrection Leon Morris observes:

We should not overlook the transformation of the disciples in all this. As noted before, they were beaten and dispirited men at the crucifixion, but they were ready to go to prison and even die for the sake of Jesus shortly afterwards.[11]

He asks, "Why the change?" Simply this, he answers, the disciples were certain of the resurrection. While this answer may be a valid apologetic for the resurrection, it does not and cannot account for the psychological transformation of the disciples. According to Luke, the gift of the Spirit to the disciples on the day of Pentecost (Acts 2:4; cf 4:8; 4:31) is alone the sufficient cause.

As transforming as this experience proved to be, it was not given for its own sake. Pentecost can best be interpreted against the wider backdrop of similar dramatic experiences in the lives of various leaders.[12] While Moses shepherds his father's-in-law flock one day, an unusual sight arrests his attention, a "bush was burning with fire, yet the bush was not consumed" (Exodus 3:2). Moses turns aside at this sight and encounters "the God of Abraham, the God of Isaac, and the God of Jacob" (Exodus 3:6). Climaxing and giving meaning to this encounter, comes the charge, "Therefore, come now, and I will send you to Pharaoh" (Exodus 3:10). It is similar for Isaiah's vision of the Lord in the Temple (Isaiah 6:1ff). This vision of the Lord enthroned in the Temple prepares Isaiah for a positive response to the question, "Whom shall I send, and who will go for us?" (Isaiah 6:8). God answers Isaiah's "Here am I. Send me!" with "Go, and tell this people" (Isaiah 6:9). And so it is with Saul's encounter with the risen Lord (Acts 9:1ff). Having confronted Saul on the road to Damascus, Jesus instructs him, "Rise, and enter the city, and it shall be told you what you must do" (Acts 9:6). The Lord then reveals to Ananias, who is also instructed to go and visit Saul, that Saul will "bear My name before the Gentiles and kings and the sons of Israel" (Acts 9:15). The true significance of these encounters is not to be found in the dramatic experiences of the burning bush, the vision of the Lord in the Temple, or in the blinding light of the risen Jesus. It is to be found in the call which climaxed the experience, "I will send you," "Go," "Bear my name before the Gentiles."

Pentecost is analogous to the experience of Moses, Isaiah, and Paul. The gift of the Spirit at Pentecost equipped the disciples for service. The phenomena which accompany the outpouring of the Spirit have no independent role. These phenomena, particularly the tongues-speaking, are not a religious experience which can be divorced from the commission of Jesus to the disciples, "You shall be my witnesses" (Acts 1:8). Pentecost differs from the experience of Moses, Isaiah, and Paul only in that it follows the earlier commissioning of the disciples, whereas for the others it precedes their call. These accompanying phenomena are not merely incidental, however, for they serve to give the experiential attestation which confirms the divine commissioning. The disciples forthcoming role as witnesses, not the profound and moving experience of tongues-speaking, is the key to understanding the significance of the gift of the Spirit on the day of Pentecost.

In common with Luke's infancy and inauguration narratives, the Pentecost narrative has typological, programmatic, and paradigmatic elements. For example, the inaugural "anointing" of Jesus is a type of the inaugural "Spirit baptism-filling" of the disciples. Similarly, the transfer of the Spirit of God from Moses to the elders is a type of the transfer of the Holy Spirit from Jesus to the disciples. Moreover, the Pentecost narrative is programmatic for the geographic and racial extension of the gospel and the complementary geographic and racial extension of the gift of the Spirit. Finally, the gift of the charismatic-prophetic Spirit on the day of Pentecost is paradigmatic for the experience of the eschatological people of God. In specific terms, they have become prophets—they have become a charismatic community.

In our study of the Pentecost narrative, we have observed that the gift of the Spirit on the day of Pentecost is a complex phenomenon. A fivefold description illuminates the meaning of the Pentecost event. It is at once a clothing, a baptizing, an empowering, a filling, and an outpouring of the Holy Spirit. No single term adequately denotes the meaning of the gift of the Spirit, but each term in this multiplex description makes its own unique contribution to the total meaning of the Pentecost event.

As Luke tells the story of Pentecost, the gift of the Holy Spirit to the disciples stands in continuity with both the charismatic activity of the Spirit in Old Testament times and with the ministry of Jesus. Four of the five terms by which Luke describes the gift of the Spirit are typical Old Testament (LXX) terms for describing the activity of the Spirit of God. The three spectacular phenomena which accompany the outpouring of the Spirit, furthermore, direct us to events in Israel's early history under Moses. The activity of the Spirit in the ministries of John and Jesus, moreover, parallels the gift of the Spirit to the disciples. Thus, the gift of the Spirit on the day of Pentecost is a pivotal event in the ongoing history of the charismatic activity of the Spirit among the people of God.

Our investigation of the Pentecost narrative, therefore, leads us to reject conventional interpretations of Pentecost, namely, that the gift of the Spirit on the day of Pentecost means the institution or birth of the Church and a complementary initiation or incorporation of the disciples into the Church. This interpretation results from either emphasizing the discontinuity between the periods of Israel, Jesus, and the Church[13] or from attributing a soteriological rather than a charismatic significance to the gift of the Spirit.[14] As a necessary corrective to the over emphasis on the discontinuity between these periods, Jacob Jervell observes:

> Luke never had any conception of the church as the new or true Israel. Luke is rather concerned to show that when the gospel was preached, the one people of God, Israel, was split in two. The result is that those Jews who do not accept the gospel are purged from Israel; the history of the people of God, of the one and only Israel, continues among obedient Jews who believe in Jesus. The promises given to Israel are fulfilled among the Jewish Christians.[15]

We have demonstrated, furthermore, that in Luke's charismatic theology Jesus, the charismatic Christ, launches the mission of the disciples with the gift of the Spirit, rather than creating the Church.

If we have interpreted Luke's Pentecost narrative correctly, then the gift of the Spirit is not for salvation, but it is for witness and service. In other words, with the transfer of the Spirit to the disciples on the day of Pentecost, they become a charismatic community, heirs to the earlier charismatic ministry of Jesus.

CHAPTER FIVE

The Holy Spirit in the Acts of the Apostles: The Charismatic Community in Mission

In fulfillment of the programmatic and paradigmatic elements in the Pentecost narrative, Acts is the story of the geographic and racial advance of the gospel. It is also the dramatic story of the complementary gift of the Holy Spirit. Subsequent to the outpouring of the Spirit on the day of Pentecost, the gift of the Spirit to the Samaritan believers, Saul, the household of Cornelius, and the disciples at Ephesus dominates Luke's record of the charismatic activity of the Spirit (Acts 8:14–19; 9:17–18; 10:44–46; 19:1–7). In addition, other bestowals of the Spirit punctuate the narrative of Acts. For example, the Spirit is given for a second time to the congregation of disciples at Jerusalem and also to the disciples at Iconium (4:31; 13:52). Moreover, the Holy Spirit initiates, directs, and empowers every advance of the gospel throughout the empire.

In the charismatic theology of St. Luke, these post-Pentecost outpourings of the Holy Spirit actualize and illustrate the universality of the prophethood of believers about which Peter spoke in his Pentecost address. The prophetic gift of the Spirit effects the charismatic calling and equipping of these various groups for vocation or service in the advance of the gospel. The Acts of the Apostles, then, is Luke's record of the charismatic community in mission.

First, we will examine the gift of the Spirit to the Samaritan believers, Saul, the household of Cornelius, and the Ephesian disciples. In addition, we will survey the other data relating to the Holy Spirit in the Acts of the Apostles.

1. The Gift of the Spirit at Samaria (8:14–19)

For many interpreters of Acts Luke's account of the evangelization of the Samaritans by Philip is an anomaly. Many Samaritans respond to

63

Philip's preaching; they believe and are baptized (8:12). In time a report reaches the apostles in Jerusalem that Samaria "had received the word of God" (8:14). Upon hearing this good news, Peter and John come down to Samaria but discover that the Holy Spirit "had not yet fallen upon any of them; they had simply been baptized in the name of the Lord Jesus" (8:16). Peter and John then pray "that they might receive the Holy Spirit" (8:15). The narrative continues, "Then they *began* laying their hands on them, and they were receiving the Holy Spirit" (8:17). This narrative describes an apparent self-contradiction—believers who had not received the Spirit.

The Samaritan narrative confronts the reader with the chronological separation between the belief of the Samaritans and their reception of the Spirit. Not only did their faith fail to effect the reception of the Spirit, but their baptism likewise failed to be the locus of their reception of the Spirit. This is a vexing theological problem for many interpreters for it contradicts their theological presuppositions concerning the baptism in the Holy Spirit. James D. G. Dunn's analysis of the Samaritan situation is typical of many interpretations. He writes:

The problem is that in the context of the rest of the NT these facts appear to be mutually exclusive and wholly irreconcilable. If they believed and were baptized (v. 12) in the name of the Lord Jesus (v. 16) they must be called Christians. But if they did not receive the Holy Spirit till later they cannot be called Christians until that time (most explicitly Rom 8:9).[1]

His solution to this apparent anomaly is to postulate that the response and commitment of the Samaritans was defective.[2] He concludes:

The NT way is rather to say: Because the Spirit has not been given, therefore the conditions [of salvation] have not been met. This is why Luke puts so much emphasis on the Samaritans' reception of the Spirit (vv. 15–20), for it is God's giving of the Spirit which makes a man a Christian, and, in the last analysis, nothing else.[3]

Reflecting as it does the methodological errors which we have exposed in chapter 1, such a contrived interpretation fails to come to grips with Luke's theology of the gift of the Spirit.

As became evident from our investigation of the Pentecost narrative, the gift of the Spirit in Luke's perspective differs from Paul's perspective (Romans 8:9). For Luke, the gift of the Spirit has a vocational purpose and equips the disciples for service. Thus, it is devoid of any soteriological connotations and, contra Dunn, it does not mean that "it is God's giving of the Spirit which makes a man a Christian." In spite of interpretations to the contrary, in Acts the Spirit is given to those who are already Christians, that is, to disciples (19:1) and believers (8:12, 19:2). Because the gift of the Spirit is charismatic or vocational and is bestowed upon believers, then the temporal separation between belief and the reception of the Spirit, as is evident in the Samaritan narrative, poses no theological inconsistency or contradiction. The problem is with the presuppositions of the commentators and is not with Luke's narrative. In fact, such a temporal separation is typical of the outpourings of the Spirit in Acts, though the experience of Cornelius demonstrates that it may be concurrent with conversion.

What does the gift of the Spirit mean for the believers at Samaria? In Luke's perspective, it does not effect their incorporation into the Church, complete the alleged initiatory complex of repentance, water baptism, and the reception of the Spirit, or simply normalize relations between Samaritans and Jews. Rather, the gift of the Spirit to the Samaritans has the same two functions as the outpouring of the Spirit to the disciples on the day of Pentecost. First, the laying on of hands by the Apostles gives to the Samaritans the same concrete attestation to the reality of the Spirit as did the signs of wind, fire, and tongues-speaking to the disciples. The reception of the Spirit is more than an affirmation of faith and is personally confirmed to each one by the laying on of hands. Second, the gift of the Spirit equips the Samaritans for discipleship. Though Jesus had commissioned the disciples prior to Pentecost and equipped them at Pentecost, the missionary task is not to be their exclusive prerogative. The gift of the Spirit to the believers at Samaria demonstrates that all, even a despised group like the Samaritans, are to engage in the missionary task. For this common responsibility they receive the same equipment —the vocational gift of the Spirit.

2. The Gift of the Spirit to Saul (9:17–18)

As a zealous pharisee and determined persecutor of the disciples of Jesus, Saul sets out for Damascus with authority to arrest and extradite any of the Way whom he might find there. Enroute, a heavenly antagonist smites Saul with a blinding light and instructs him, "Rise, and enter the city, and it shall be told you what you must do" (9:6). Meanwhile, in Damascus the Lord instructs a disciple, Ananias by name, "Go [to Saul], for he is a chosen instrument of Mine, to bear My name before the Gentiles and kings and the sons of Israel" (9:15). With reluctant obedience Ananias seeks out Saul "and after laying his hands on him said, 'Brother Saul, the Lord Jesus . . . has sent me so that you may regain your sight, and be filled with the Holy Spirit'" (9:17). The narrative continues, "And immediately there fell from his eyes something like scales, and he regained his sight, and he arose and was baptized" (9:18).

This narrative brings together two characteristic Lukan motifs: vocational ability and the gift of the Spirit. In describing Saul's encounter with the risen Lord Luke emphasizes his calling not his conversion. The stress falls upon what Saul must do, to bear the name of Jesus before the Gentiles. Zeal may have provided sufficient motivation for Saul the persecutor, but it was inadequate for his new vocation in life. For his unprecedented mission, his vocation to the Gentiles, he needed the gift of the Spirit, just as surely as the disciples needed it for their mission to the Jews. Thus, "filled with the Spirit" is the necessary complement to the charge, "bear My name before the Gentiles."

Luke does not mention either the moment of Saul's being filled with the Spirit or any phenomena which may have accompanied the event. Those who believe that the Spirit is given in water baptism naturally interpret Luke's statement, "and he arose and was baptized," to describe the locus of his Spirit-filling. But to this interpretation it may be objected that the narrative gives just as good grounds for associating Saul's Spirit-filling with Ananias laying his hands upon him. Others interpret Paul's statement to the Corinthian church, "I thank God, I speak in tongues more than you all" (1 Corinthians 14:18), to imply that Paul must have spoken in tongues when he was filled with the Spirit. While it is true that all of these suggestions are possible, none is demonstrable. Luke's silence makes it clear that he can be quite indifferent to both the timing and the phenomena associated with the gift of the Spirit. It is equally evident that Luke's primary concern is with the fact of God's calling and His equipping. Thus, the gift of the Spirit to Saul has the same two-pronged emphasis as the gift of the Spirit to the disciples on the day of Pentecost and the believers at Samaria: vocational ability and the gift of the Spirit.

Significantly, Luke parallels the charismatic experience of both Peter and Paul. This parallelism may be summarized as follows:

	Peter	Paul
Filled with the Holy Spirit	Acts 2:4; 4:8; 4:31	Acts 9:17; 13:9; 13:52
Guidance from the Holy Spirit	Acts 10:19–20	Acts 13:1–2; 16:6–7; 21:4, 10–11
Instruments for Gift of Holy Spirit	Acts 8:15–17	Acts 19:6

This parallelism shows Paul's experience of the Spirit to be authentic and accredits his apostleship to the Gentiles.

3. The Gift of the Spirit to the Household of Cornelius (10:44–46)

Visions, first to Cornelius and later to Peter, combine to bring about the visit of Peter to this Roman centurion. As Peter recites the history of God's saving acts in Jesus of Nazareth, "the Holy Spirit fell upon all those who were listening to the message" (10:44). Manifesting the gift of the Spirit, which has been poured out upon them, they begin "speaking with tongues and exalting God" (10:46). From this unexpected outburst of tongues-speaking, Peter concludes that the household of Cornelius has received the Holy Spirit just as the disciples had on the day of Pentecost and orders "them to be baptized in the name of Jesus Christ" (10:48).

For interpreting the gift of the Spirit to the household of Cornelius, Luke directs his readers to the Pentecost narrative. First, Luke uses similar terminology in both narratives: tongues-speaking (2:4; 10:46) and exalting God (2:11; 10:46). Second, Peter explicitly identifies the gift of the Spirit to Cornelius with Pentecost. When defending his visit to Cornelius before the Jerusalem church Peter testifies that "the Holy Spirit fell upon them, just as he did upon us at the beginning" (11:15). Some years later Peter testifies to the Jerusalem council that God gave the Holy Spirit to Cornelius, "just as He also did to us" (15:8). One conclusion is inescapable: the gift of the Spirit to the household of Cornelius has the same vocational or charismatic purpose as the gift of the Spirit to the disciples on the day of Pentecost.

In addition to the vocational purpose of the gift, the Cornelius narrative emphasizes the testimonial function of the gift. In the first place, the outpouring of the Spirit is dramatic testimony to Peter and his companions. From Cornelius' account of how he came to send for Peter they had already learned the lesson that God does not show partiality (10:34) and that he welcomes all God-fearers (10:35). The outpouring of the Spirit teaches them a new lesson, namely, that God's impartiality applies to more than just salvation, it applies to all His gifts. The household of Cornelius receives the same prophetic gift of the Spirit which they as the uniquely chosen disciples had received on the day of Pentecost. In the second place, the outpouring of the Spirit is dramatic testimony to Cornelius and his household that God makes no distinction between himself and the Jews: that is, that they can receive the prophetic gift of the Spirit without having to convert to Judaism.

4. The Gift of the Spirit to the Disciples at Ephesus (19:1–7)

On his second missionary journey Paul finds a group of about twelve disciples in the city of Ephesus. He enquires, "Did you receive the Holy Spirit when you believed?" (19:2). They reply in the negative, receive fuller exposition concerning Jesus, and are baptized in the name of the Lord Jesus (19:3–5). Climaxing the narrative, "when Paul had laid his hands upon them, the Holy Spirit came on them, and they *began* speaking with tongues and prophesying" (19:6).

This narrative has the same ingredients as the Samaritan narrative: disciples who have believed and yet not received the Holy Spirit. Two facts—Paul knows that all Christians have the Spirit (Romans 8:9), and he knows that in spite of the limited content of their faith these disciples are Christians[4]—mean that his question, "Did you receive the Holy Spirit when you believed?" is not in an initiatory or soteriological context. The context of his question is clear from the solution, which is an outburst of tongues and prophecy. There can be no doubt that Paul is asking nothing more nor less than whether they have received the prophetic gift of the Spirit. Dunn's interpretation of this narrative demonstrates that he fails to understand either Luke or Paul. He writes, "The twelve Ephesians are therefore further examples of men who were not far short of Christianity, but were not yet Christians because they lacked the vital factor—the Holy Spirit."[5] There is no tension between the fact of the indwelling of the Holy Spirit in the life of every believer and an additional experience of receiving the prophetic or charismatic gift of the Spirit.

Having surveyed Luke's record of the gift of the Spirit to the believers at Samaria, Saul, the household of Cornelius, and the disciples at Ephesus, we are now in a position to answer the question: What is Luke's purpose in these narratives? Two purposes are evident; the first is historical and the second is theological. First, these narratives illustrate the historical fulfillment of the commission which Jesus gave to the disciples before His ascension to extend the gospel throughout the empire (1:8). Second, they illustrate the universality of the vocational gift of the Spirit. Wherever and to whomever the gospel spreads, God also pours out the gift of the Spirit for vocational purposes; it is neither localized in Jerusalem nor restricted to Jewish Christians. This is consistent with the purpose of the gift of the Spirit to the disciples on the day of Pentecost, which Peter interprets in universalistic terms. In conclusion, these narratives illustrate the charismatic character of the Church, for everywhere it receives the vocational gift of the Spirit.

5. The Means of Conferring the Holy Spirit

Studies of the gift of the Spirit in Acts often raise the question of the means by which God bestows the Spirit. Typically, the discussion focuses on the relationship between water baptism, the laying on of hands, and the reception of the Spirit.[6] It is also suggested that prayer is the means through which the Spirit is given.[7]

In Acts, the Spirit is nowhere conferred through water baptism. There is a loose association between the gift of the Spirit and water baptism in but three narratives: the gift of the Spirit follows the water baptism of the believers at Samaria (8:12–17), it precedes and is the basis for the water baptism of the household of Cornelius (10:44–48), and it follows the water baptism of the disciples at Ephesus (19:4–6). More numerous are those bestowals of the Spirit which take place entirely apart from water baptism. For example, in the book of Acts there is Pentecost (2:1ff), Peter (4:8), the Jerusalem church (4:31), Paul (13:9), and the disciples at Iconium (13:52). In Luke's Gospel there are the examples of Elizabeth and Zacharias (Luke 1:41, 67).

Acts 2:38 is the classic text on which is built the doctrine that the Holy Spirit is conferred through the mode of water baptism. Peter's promise of the gift of the Spirit must be interpreted against the outpouring of the Spirit which Peter and the other disciples have just experienced. Hence, Peter's promise of the Spirit can only be the promise of the eschatological gift of the Spirit, which in fulfillment of Joel's promise is particularly the prophetic or charismatic gift of the Spirit. In the immediate context of his own reception of the Spirit, Peter's promise of the Spirit thus lacks any initiation/incorporation connotations. What Peter does make clear is that the gift of the Spirit is only for the penitent; that is, for disciples of Jesus.

On three occasions the gift of the Spirit is associated with the laying on of hands (8:17; 9:17; 19:6). This procedure has an Old Testament precedent in the gift of the Spirit to Joshua (Deuteronomy 34:9). However, as it became evident with water baptism, the Holy Spirit is bestowed most often apart from any specific means, including the laying on of hands. This fact is fatal to the doctrine that the Holy Spirit is conferred in Confirmation.

It has recently been suggested that prayer, rather than water baptism or the laying on of hands, is the means by which the power of the Spirit is historically realized. Undeniably, prayer has an important association with the gift of the Spirit. (Luke 3:21, Acts 1:14; 2:1ff; 4:31; 8:15). However, rather than being the means for conferring the Holy Spirit, prayer is more properly the spiritual environment in which the Spirit is often bestowed.

The complex record of the gift of the Holy Spirit in Luke-Acts rebukes all attempts to formulate a monolithic doctrine of the means by which the Holy Spirit is conferred. All must admit that "Nowhere is it claimed in Acts that baptism of itself, or the laying on of hands as such, or even a combination of them both, confers or can confer the Spirit."[8] Rather, in these narratives, "the freedom of the Spirit is strongly emphasized."[9] Luke's primary concern is with the fact of the gift of the Spirit and not with any real or imagined means through which the Holy Spirit is conferred.

It is clear that to state the problem of the means by which the Holy Spirit is conferred in the above terms reflects a fundamental misunderstanding of Luke's theology of the Holy Spirit. We have demonstrated that, for Luke, the Holy Spirit is given to those who are already disciples or believers and that the purpose of the gift of the Spirit is charismatic or vocational. Therefore, we conclude that Luke's descriptions of the gift of the Spirit make the discussion of the means for conferring the Spirit irrelevant for understanding Luke's theology of the Holy Spirit.

6. Miscellaneous Texts

In addition to emphasizing the gift of the Spirit to the believers at Samaria, Saul, the household of Cornelius, and the disciples at Ephesus, Luke also records a diverse but general activity of the Spirit throughout Acts. It is to these further data that we now turn our attention. The rich and varied cognate terminology for the gift of the Spirit requires some comment, as does Luke's consistent use of the passive and active voices for his terminology: filled with the Holy Spirit and received the Holy Spirit. We will also examine the role of the Holy Spirit in witness or mission.

A. Cognate Terminology

Since the gift of the Holy Spirit in Acts is vocational, then related terminology must have a similar meaning in the same context. Thus, terminology such as: the promise of the Father (1:4), the promise of the Holy Spirit (2:33), the gift of the Holy Spirit (2:38; 10:45), and the gift of God (8:20) describe the vocational gift of the Holy Spirit.

When describing the gift of the Spirit, Luke consistently uses one of two phrases "filled with the Holy Spirit" (see chart p. 53) and "received the Holy Spirit" (1:8; 8:15; 10:47; 19:2). He is also consistent in using "filled with the Holy Spirit" in the passive voice and "received the Holy Spirit" in the active voice. Because they are in the middle voice, which describes an action that the subject performs for himself, the two exceptions to this pattern do not effect the distinction that Luke makes between being filled in the passive and receiving in the active voice.

This is an important and interesting distinction. The passive voice signifies that the subject of the verb is being acted upon, or is the recipient of the action. In the context of the gift of the Spirit, God acts upon the believer, and fills him with the Holy Spirit. The active voice signifies that the subject of the verb produces the action. Thus, the believer must respond in order to receive the Holy Spirit. On those occasions when the disciples are filled with the Holy Spirit, Luke emphasizes the divine initiative. On those occasions when the disciples receive the Holy Spirit, he emphasizes the concomitant human response to that initiative. Luke makes it clear that God does not arbitrarily impose His Spirit upon the disciples apart from their response to His initiative. He also makes it clear that no one can take from God what He has not first given. In Luke's perspective, "received the Holy Spirit" is the necessary complement to being "filled with the Holy Spirit."

B. The Holy Spirit and Mission

Before His ascension, Jesus associates the Holy Spirit with witness or mission when He promises the disciples, "but you shall receive power when the Holy Spirit has come upon you; and you shall be My witnesses both in Jerusalem, and in all Judea and Samaria, and even to the remotest part of the earth" (1:8). The initial fulfillment of this promise follows the outpouring of the Spirit on the day of Pentecost. Peter seizes the opportunity presented by the crowd-attracting phenomena and witnesses to the curious pilgrims (2:14–40). So effective is his Spirit-empowered witness that on that day about three thousand are added to the company of disciples (2:41). Somewhat later, Peter and John are arrested and brought before the Sanhedrin. In fulfillment of an earlier promise made by Jesus (Luke 12:11—12), Peter is filled with the Holy Spirit and gives powerful witness to them (4:8–20). After being further threatened by the Sanhedrin, they are released and rejoin the company of disciples. And when they prayed, ''they were all filled with the Holy Spirit, and began to speak the word of God with boldness'' (4:31).

Not only do the disciples witness in Jerusalem by the power and inspiration of the Spirit, but ''Every initiative in evangelism recorded in Acts is the initiative of the Holy Spirit.''[10] Two such occasions occur in the missionary activity of Philip. The encounter between Philip and the Ethiopian eunuch is no happenstance, as Luke records:

But an angel of the Lord spoke to Philip saying, ''Arise and go south to the road that descends from Jerusalem to Gaza.'' (This is a desert *road*.) And he arose and went; and behold, there was an Ethiopian eunuch, a court official of Candace. . . . And the Spirit said to Philip, ''Go up and join this chariot.'' (8:26–29).

After Philip had baptized the Ethiopian:

The Spirit of the Lord snatched Philip away; and the eunuch saw him no more, but went on his way rejoicing. But Philip found himself at Azotus; and as he passed through he kept preaching the gospel to all the cities, until he came to Caesarea (8:39–40).

Here, as elsewhere in Acts, Luke identifies the Holy Spirit with the angel of the Lord and the Spirit of the Lord.

It is certain that Peter would never have visited Cornelius apart from God's intervention. First, Peter receives a vision and is commanded to eat the ceremonially unclean food which he sees. This object lesson teaches Peter that he may fellowship with a Gentile. Second, the Holy Spirit instructs Peter to do this very thing. Luke reports that, ''while Peter was reflecting on the vision, the Spirit said to him, 'Behold, three men are looking for you. But arise, go downstairs, and accompany them without misgivings; for I have sent them Myself'' (10:19–20).

Like Philip and Peter before him, Paul also experiences the guidance of the Holy Spirit. The first occurrence of the Spirit's guidance launches his missionary career. During an Antiochian prayer meeting of certain prophets and teachers, the Holy Spirit instructs, ''Set apart for Me Barnabas and Saul for the work to which I have called them'' (13:2). The initiative and guidance of the Spirit continues to characterize the missionary activity of Paul. On his second missionary journey, Paul proposes to preach the gospel in Asia. However, the Holy Spirit intervenes. Luke reports:

And they passed through the Phrygian and Galatian region, having been forbidden by the Holy Spirit to speak the word in Asia; and when they had come to Mysia, they were trying to go into Bithynia, and the Spirit of Jesus did not permit them; and passing by Mysia, they came down to Troas (16:6–8).

As a result of this leading of the Spirit, Paul sails for Macedonia and brings the gospel to Europe. Considerably later, Paul begins his final journey to Jerusalem under the compulsion of the Spirit. He testifies to the Ephesian elders, "And now, behold, bound in spirit, I am on my way to Jerusalem" (20:22).

From these accounts of the missionary activity of Philip, Peter, and Paul, it is evident that the Holy Spirit initiates and directs every missionary thrust.

Of the five major accounts of the gift of the Holy Spirit in Acts, the Pentecost narrative takes pride of place. Moreover, it also guides us in our interpretation of the gift of the Spirit to the Samaritans, Saul, Cornelius, and the Ephesians. As in the Pentecost narrative, so in these subsequent narratives, the gift of the Spirit is vocational. These narratives demonstrate that all who receive the gospel, either simultaneously or subsequently, also receive the charismatic gift of the Spirit. Thus, the gift of the Spirit to the Samaritans, Saul, Cornelius, and the Ephesians are historical examples of Peter's Pentecost interpretation: the vocational gift of the Spirit is potentially universal.

In addition to these five narratives, references to the Holy Spirit pervade the record of Acts. Luke's characteristic use of the phrases "filled with the Holy Spirit" and "received the Holy Spirit" describe the complementary roles of the divine initiative and the human response to that initiative. Moreover, the variety of terms which Luke uses all describe the charismatic activity of the Spirit and not initiation or incorporation. Like John and Jesus before them, the charismatic community of disciples is Spirit-empowered and Spirit-directed for its missionary task.

CHAPTER SIX

The Charismatic Theology of St. Luke: Synthesis and Challenge

In comparison to the varied literature of the New Testament, Luke-Acts is unique. It stands alone as the only two-volumed book in the New Testament. More importantly, it is the only *heilsgeschichte*—history of salvation—in the New Testament. As we have observed, however, Luke is more than the historian of New Testament times; he is also a theologian in his own right. In his historical-theological perspective, the two complementary themes of "salvation" and "the charismatic activity of the Holy Spirit" dominate Luke-Acts. Thus, in addition to classifying Luke-Acts as *heilsgeschichte*, it may also be classified as *pneumageschichte*[1]—the story of both the charismatic Christ and the charismatic community of disciples in mission.

Part One: A Synthesis of Luke's Charismatic Theology

1. The Charismatic Theology of Luke-Acts as Heir to the Charismatic Theology of the Old Testament

It is against this background of charismatic leadership in Israel, of the prophetic hope for the coming of the Lord's anointed and for a community which will receive both the charismatic gift of the Spirit and the indwelling of the Spirit, that the gift of the Holy Spirit in Luke-Acts is to be interpreted.

A. *The Spirit and the Messianic Age: Fulfillment in Luke-Acts*

The activity of the Spirit is a central theme in the two inauguration narratives of Luke-Acts. In the Gospel, the widespread activity of the Spirit in the opening narrative finds its climax in the descent of the Holy Spirit upon Jesus at His baptism by John (Luke 3:21–22). Similarly, in

Acts the inauguration narrative focuses upon the gift of the Spirit to the disciples on the day of Pentecost (Acts 2:4).

Both of these narratives emphasize that the gift of the Holy Spirit fulfills prophecy. For His synagogue homily after His baptism, Jesus interprets His baptismal experience in terms of an oracle from the prophet Isaiah, declaring, "Today this Scripture has been fulfilled in your hearing" (Luke 4:21). Similarly, Peter claims that the experience of the disciples on the day of Pentecost fulfills an oracle from Joel. He announces, "but this is what was spoken of through the prophet Joel" (Acts 2:16). Of all the evangelists, Luke alone records this consciousness in Jesus and the disciples that they have received the Holy Spirit in fulfillment of prophecy. Luke's record of this appeal to the prophets demonstrates that in the experience of the early church and the theology of Luke the last days have now dawned in the successive ministries of Jesus and the disciples.

Moreover, in appealing to the prophets, Jesus and the disciples express their conviction that the gift of the Spirit is a charismatic or vocational experience. That is, the Holy Spirit is upon Jesus anointing Him to preach the gospel and subsequently upon the disciples causing them to prophesy. It is noteworthy that in identifying the gift of the Spirit on the day of Pentecost with the prophecy of Joel, rather than quoting from one of the numerous prophetic references to the indwelling and inward renewal of the Spirit, Peter cites the only prophetic text which explicitly speaks of a charismatic outpouring of the Spirit upon the community of God's people.

B. Septuagintal Terminology in Luke-Acts

In comparison with John and Paul, Luke has a distinctive terminology for the activity of the Holy Spirit. Absent in Luke-Acts is such characteristic Johannine terminology as "the Spirit of truth" and "the Paraclete." Also absent is typical Pauline terminology such as "the fruit of the Spirit," "the gifts of the Spirit," and "the seal of the Spirit." Not only is characteristic Johannine and Pauline terminology absent in the writings of Luke, but common Lukan terminology is either absent or rare in the Johannine and Pauline literature. Reflecting a different heritage than do both John and Paul, Luke commonly describes the activity of the Holy Spirit in septuagintal terminology.

This influence of the Septuagint upon Luke's terminology for the activity of the Holy Spirit is shown in Chapter 2. These data which we have outlined lead to two conclusions. In the first place, while Luke does not limit himself to septuagintal terminology, he is clearly a debtor to the Greek Bible for his most distinctive terminology by which he describes the activity of the Holy Spirit. However, though Luke is indebted to the Septuagint for much of his terminology, he is not a slavish imitator. Rather, he creatively describes the activity of the Holy Spirit in New Testament times in terms of his scriptural and theological heritage. In the second place, this septuagintal terminology in Luke-Acts describes the same kind of experience for Luke as it did for the translators of the Septuagint. This is the charismatic activity of the Spirit among the company of God's people. Consequently, this terminology does not describe what contemporary interpreters term to be initiation or incorporation.

C. Charismatic Motifs

The transfer of the Spirit motif, so characteristic of Old Testament times, is also prominent in Luke-Acts, particularly in the transfer of the Holy Spirit from Jesus to the disciples. Though the Gospel opens with an unexpected outburst of the activity of the Holy Spirit from Jesus' baptism to His ascension, the Spirit is concentrated solely upon Jesus. As Luke reports it, He is full of the Holy Spirit, led by the Spirit, and ministers in the power of the Spirit (Luke 4:1, 14). Luke's record is reminiscent of the programmatic descriptions of the gift of the Spirit to Moses and Elijah and makes explicit what is implicit in Jesus' claim to messiahship—He is the unique bearer of the Spirit.

Having become the Lord's anointed or unique bearer of the Spirit at His baptism, Jesus becomes the giver of the Spirit to the disciples on the day of Pentecost. This transfer of the Spirit from the risen and exalted Lord to his disciples is strikingly similar to the transfer of the Spirit from Moses to the elders. Both involve a transfer of the Spirit from an individual to a group. Moreover, in both cases the transfer of the Spirit results in an outburst of prophecy. This transfer of the Spirit to the disciples on the day of Pentecost potentially fulfills Moses' desire that all God's people might be prophets, for with the gift of the Spirit to the disciples the age of the prophethood of all believers has dawned.

Because the day of Pentecost represents a transfer of the Spirit from Jesus to the disciples, it must have a similar meaning for them as it did for the baptismal gift of the Spirit to Jesus. Though Luke uses different terminology in each narrative, the gift of the Spirit to the disciples is

functionally equivalent to the anointing of Jesus by the Spirit, inaugurating and empowering their respective ministries. Consequently,
as it was in Old Testament times and for the ministry of Jesus, the gift of
the Spirit to the disciples on the day of Pentecost is primarily vocational
in both purpose and result.

The transfer of the Holy Spirit also takes place subsequent to the day
of Pentecost. In Samaria, Simon saw that the Spirit was given through
(διά) the laying on of the apostles' hands (Acts 8:18). In Damascus,
Ananias laid his hands on Saul so that he might see again and be filled
with the Holy Spirit (Acts 9:17). At Ephesus, when Paul placed his
hands on the disciples, the Holy Spirit came on them, and they spoke in
tongues and prophesied (Acts 19:6). The gift of the Spirit to the household of Cornelius, which is independent of the imposition of hands, is
reminiscent of the transfer of the Spirit from Moses to the leaders.

Not only is the Old Testament transfer motif characteristic of the gift
of the Holy Spirit in Luke-Acts, but the complementary sign motif is
also prominent in Luke-Acts. Luke does not, however, use the septuagintal sign terminology. Nevertheless, the sign motif is evident in the
visible and audible phenomena which accompany the gift of the Holy
Spirit. For example, Matthew, Mark, and John simply report that the
Spirit descended "like a dove" (Matthew 3:16, Mark 1:10, John 1:32),
whereas Luke reports that the Spirit descended "in bodily form, as a
dove" (Luke 3:22). By this qualification Luke emphasizes that the
descent of the Spirit upon Jesus is not visionary; it is an external,
physical, and objective manifestation of the Spirit. Concomitant with
the descent of the Spirit and the voice from heaven, then, are the visible
and audible signs which attest to the anointing or messiahship of Jesus.

Just as the anointing of Jesus is attested to by visible and audible
signs, so the transfer of the Holy Spirit to the disciples on the day of
Pentecost is also attested to by visible and audible signs. Luke reports:

And suddenly there came from heaven a noise like a violent, rushing wind, and it filled
the whole house where they were sitting. And there appeared to them tongues as of fire
distributing themselves, they rested on each one of them. And they were all filled with the
Holy Spirit and began to speak with other tongues, as the Spirit was giving them utterance
(Acts 2:2-4).

The visible sign is the tongues of fire and the audible signs are the
sounds of the wind and the disciples' speaking with other tongues. As
Peter observes in his Pentecost address, the transfer of the Spirit is an
experience which the crowd could both "see and hear" (Acts 2:33).

The sign motif is also characteristic of Luke's record of the gift of the Holy Spirit to the Samaritans, the household of Cornelius and the Ephesians. After the Samaritans had received the Holy Spirit, Simon, "saw that the Spirit was bestowed through the laying on of the apostles' hands" (Acts 8:18). Having heard the household of Cornelius speaking in tongues, "the circumcised believers from among the circumcised . . . were amazed, because the gift of the Holy Spirit had been poured out upon the Gentiles," also (Acts 10:45). Peter subsequently reports that God "bore witness to them (ἐμαρτυρησεν), giving them the Holy Spirit, just as He also did to us" (Acts 15:8). Similarly, the Holy Spirit came upon the disciples at Ephesus, "and they *began* speaking with tongues and prophesying" (Acts 19:6). Luke's repeated emphasis on "seeing" and "hearing" demonstrates the centrality of the sign motif for his theology of the Holy Spirit. In his terminology, the visible and/or audible phenomena "witness" to the gift of the Spirit.

2. The Charismatic Theology of Luke-Acts as Unique in Comparison to the Charismatic Theology of the Old Testament.

Though the vocational gift of the Holy Spirit in Luke-Acts is in continuity with Old Testament times, nevertheless, significant differences distinguish the activity of the Spirit in the messianic age from earlier times. In Old Testament times, and even in the Gospel era, the activity of the Spirit is restricted to chosen leaders. From Pentecost onwards, however, the vocational gift of the Spirit is potentially universal. Luke's Samaritan, Cornelius, and Ephesian narratives illustrate the universal character of the vocational gift of the Spirit. Furthermore, the Messiah supercedes the nation as the object of the vocational activity of the Spirit. For example, John is filled with the Spirit, but solely to equip him for his role as forerunner for the coming Messiah. At His baptism, Jesus becomes the unique bearer of the Spirit, and at Pentecost He becomes the giver of the Spirit. The Holy Spirit is so closely identified with the person and ministry of Jesus that He is "the Spirit of Jesus" (Acts 16:7). With the qualification that the vocational activity of the Spirit is now potentially universal and its new object is the ongoing mission of the Messiah, the gift of the Spirit is in continuity with the way in which God has always poured out His Spirit upon His servants.

Moreover, unlike Old Testament times when there is no personalization of the Spirit of God, in Luke-Acts the Holy Spirit is fully personal.

For example, the Spirit can be lied to (Acts 5:3ff) and can speak (Acts 10:19).

3. The Charismatic Dimension of the Gift of the Spirit in Luke-Acts

Luke is indebted to Jesus for his understanding of the vocational purpose of the gift of the Holy Spirit. In words programmatic for the subsequent mission of the disciples, Jesus informs them, "You shall receive power when the Holy Spirit has come upon you; and you shall be My witnesses both in Jerusalem, and in all Judea and Samaria, and even to the remotest part of the earth" (Acts 1:8). In this dominical saying Luke gives his readers the key to interpreting the purpose of the gift of the Spirit, not only to the disciples on the day of Pentecost but also throughout Luke-Acts.

If Luke's record accurately reflects the teaching of Jesus about the purpose of the gift of the Holy Spirit, then the result of receiving the Spirit will be consistent with the purpose. Where Luke records the result we have observed this to be the case, not only for the gift of the Spirit throughout Acts but also for the activity of the Spirit in the Gospel. Whether the Spirit is given to John as an unborn infant, to Jesus at the Jordan, to the disciples on the day of Pentecost, or to Saul in Damascus, the pattern is consistent: the gift of the Spirit always results in mission. Because Luke describes the gift of the Spirit to the Samaritans, the household of Cornelius, and the Ephesians in similar terms, the vocational result is implict here as well. Though we may look to Luke in vain for directives for the so-called normative Christian experience, we do encounter an invariable pattern for the gift of the Spirit in the unfolding record of the inauguration and extension of the gospel: the gift of the Spirit always precedes and effects mission or vocation.

A. Specifically, the Charismatic Gift is Prophetic

In specific terms, the charismatic gift of the Holy Spirit in Luke-Acts is often prophetic. Luke uses the term prophet(s) for John the Baptist, Anna (prophetess), Jesus, Agabus and companions, certain disciples at Antioch, Judas and Silas, and the four daughters of Philip (prophetesses). Though not designated as such by Luke, many others must certainly be understood to be prophets. This includes all those who are filled with the Spirit—Luke's technical term to describe prophetic inspiration. It also includes those such as Peter (Acts 10:19) and Paul (Acts 16:9) who experience visions and dreams, the accredited mode of prophetic revelation (Numbers 12:6; Joel 2:28ff). These prophets engage in a variety of activities throughout Luke-Acts: exhortation (Luke 3:18), miracle working (Luke 7:14–16, Acts 2:43; 3:1ff; 5:15; 6:8; 8:13; etc.), prediction (Acts 11:28; 21:10ff), judgment (Acts 8:20; 13:9), and worship (Luke 1:68, Acts 2:47; etc.). The large number of designated prophets and the relative frequency of prophecy in Luke-Acts is consistent with the universality of the prophetic activity of the Spirit in the messianic age.

B. Consecration and Empowering: Anointed/Baptized and Filled with the Spirit

As we have seen, Luke describes the gift of the Spirit by a variety of terminology; for example, filled, anointed, clothed, baptized, and empowered by the Spirit. Though these and other terms all describe the charismatic gift of the Spirit, a twofold distinction must be made. The terms "anointed" and "baptized" describe the consecrating work of the Holy Spirit in inaugurating one's public ministry. The terms "filled," "clothed," and "empowered" describe the actual equipping by the Spirit for that ministry. Here, then, is the distinction between the once-for-all and the repetitive character of the gift of the Spirit. The consecration by the Spirit is once-for-all, while, as the need arises, the equipping by the Spirit is repetitive.

4. The Charismatic Gift of the Spirit as Experiential

To the extent that Luke makes it explicit, the charismatic gift of the Holy Spirit in Luke-Acts is always an experiential phenomenon. It is so for Elizabeth, Zacharias, Jesus, the disciples on the day of Pentecost, the household of Cornelius, and the disciples at Ephesus.

Throughout Luke-Acts, then, the gift of the Spirit for vocation is never a matter of faith-perception, but it is always an experience-reality. The prejudicial attempt to drive a wedge between receiving the Spirit by faith and receiving the Spirit by experience, with the presumption that faith is superior to and independent from experience, cannot be harmonized with Luke's record of the gift of the Spirit. To despise the experiential dimension of the gift of the Spirit is in Pauline terminology to quench the Spirit (1 Thessalonians 5:19).

A fresh picture of the gift of the Holy Spirit in Luke-Acts emerges from the investigation: Luke relates the gift of the Spirit to service and witness; that is, to vocation. In other words, in Luke's theology of the

Holy Spirit the activity of the Spirit is always charismatic in both purpose and result. Luke's charismatic theology is characterized by an Old
Testament heritage, an experiential dimension, frequent prophetic
activity, and no temporal limitations. Only those who resist the evidence can continue to interpret the gift of the Holy Spirit in Luke-Acts
to be an initiation-conversion experience.

Part Two: The Challenge of Luke's Charismatic Theology

Because of their personal and theological prejudices, some interpreters will reject this exposition of Luke's theology of the Holy Spirit;
nevertheless, they will concede that Luke does have a charismatic theology. This concession is made palatable by a series of maneuvers which
enable the interpreter to avoid the implications of Luke's charismatic
theology for contemporary Christian experience. For example, interpreters may assign a *dispensational* limit to the charismatic activity
of the Spirit, limiting it to New Testament times.[2] Moreover, interpreters sometimes label this charismatic activity as *abnormal*[3] and urgently
insist that Christians are to be content with normal growth into Christian
maturity. Finally, while accepting the legitimacy of Luke's charismatic
theology, interpreters may relegate it to a *secondary* status.[4]

Though they are often clothed in the garb of profound scholarship and
sincere piety, these tactics either silence or emasculate Luke's
charismatic theology. Luke would be surprised to learn from contemporary interpreters that contrary to his charismatic theology, subsequent
generations of Christians are fully capable of ministering apart from the
charismatic empowering of the Spirit, charismatic Christianity is abnormal, and charismatic Christianity is secondary. To interpret Luke's
charismatic theology as dispensational, abnormal, and secondary,
however, reveals more about the attitudes of contemporary interpreters
and the theological and ecclesiastical traditions which they are defending than it does about the activity of the Holy Spirit in Luke-Acts.
Surely Luke's theology of the Holy Spirit demands a more worthy
response than this.

The witness of the Gospel of Luke is that by the empowering of the
Holy Spirit Jesus was a charismatic. Similarly, the witness of the Acts
of the Apostles is that the disciples were a charismatic community.
Thus, in the theology of Luke the Church is charismatic. This remains
true whether or not the Church is always conscious of its charismatic

character, or whether or not it functions at the level of its charismatic potential. Traditionally, the Church has been suspicious of charismatic experience. Though they may pay lip service to the charismatic character of the Church, in reality some Christian traditions "despise prophecies" and "quench the Spirit." In contrast, in this century Pentecostals and Charismatics have promoted the manifestation of the charismatic activity of the Holy Spirit. They have, however, often encountered bitter opposition over this.

The contemporary Church is presently at an impasse over the doctrine of the Holy Spirit. Little constructive dialogue takes place among Christians with conflicting views. Rather, to the discredit of all parties, suspicion, hostility, and intolerance characterize the relationship between those with conflicting views on the validity of the charismatic experience for today. The charismatic character of the Church makes it imperative that all traditions in the Church reassess their doctrine and experience of the Spirit in the light of Luke's charismatic theology. For example, anti-Charismatics must recognize that Luke does primarily teach a charismatic theology, and that this is a valid experience for the contemporary Church. On the other hand, Pentecostals and Charismatics must remember that the gift of the Spirit is not just a spiritual blessing; it is a responsibility. Its meaning extends beyond the prayer room and the worship service to a world which needs to hear a prophetic voice in concert with the demonstration of the power of the Spirit.

The literature of the New Testament reveals three primary dimensions of the activity of the Holy Spirit: 1) salvation, 2) sanctification, and 3) service. These dimensions are interdependent and complementary. However, in the development of Protestant theology, the Reformed tradition has emphasized the activity of the Spirit in initiation-conversion, the Wesleyan tradition has subsequently emphasized the activity of the Spirit in holiness or sanctification, and the Pentecostal tradition has finally emphasized the charismatic activity of the Spirit in worship and service. It is the sad lesson of Church history and contemporary experience that the charismatic activity of the Holy Spirit cannot flourish in a climate which is hostile or indifferent to this dimension of the activity of the Spirit. Thus, Luke's charismatic theology challenges the Reformed and the Wesleyan traditions to add the charismatic activity of the Spirit to their initiation-conversion and holiness experiences of the Spirit.

END NOTES

Chapter One

[1]L. E. Keck and J. L. Martyn, eds., *Studies in Luke–Acts* (London: S.P.C.K, 1968).
[2]W.C. van Unnik, "Luke–Acts, A Storm Center in Contemporary Scholarship," in *Studies in Luke–Acts*, ed. by L. E. Keck and J. L. Martyn (London: S.P.C.K, 1968), pp. 18–32.
[3]Influential or significant works on the Holy Spirit published in the decade of the '70s include the following: Frederick Dale Bruner, *A Theology of the Holy Spirit: The Pentecostal Experience and the New Testament Witness* (Grand Rapids: William B. Eerdmans, 1970); James D. G. Dunn, *Baptism in the Holy Spirit: A Re-examination of the New Testament Teaching of the Gift of the Spirit in relation to Pentecostalism today*, Studies in Biblical Theology, Second Series, 15 (London: SCM Press Ltd, 1970); Charles Webb Carter, *The Person and Ministry of the Holy Spirit: A Wesleyan Perspective* (Grand Rapids: Baker Book House, 1974); James D. G. Dunn, *Jesus and the Spirit: A Study of the Religious and Charismatic Experience of Jesus and the First Christians as Reflected in the New Testament*, New Testament Library (London: SCM Press Ltd, 1975); Michael Green, *I Believe in the Holy Spirit* (Grand Rapids: William B. Eerdmans, 1975); Stanley M. Horton, *What The Bible Says About The Holy Spirit* (Springfield, MO.: Gospel Publishing House, 1976); George T. Montague, *The Holy Spirit: Growth of a Biblical Tradition* (New York: Paulist Press, 1967); G. W. H. Lampe, *God As Spirit: The Bampton Lectures, 1976* (Oxford: Oxford University Press, 1977); Charles E. Hummel, *Fire in the Fireplace: Contemporary Charismatic Renewal* (Downers Grove, IL.: InterVarsity Press, 1978); L. Thomas Holdcroft, *The Holy Spirit: A Pentecostal Interpretation* (Springfield, MO.: Gospel Publishing House, 1979).
[4]John R. W. Stott, *The Baptism and Fullness of the Holy Spirit* (Downers Grove, IL.: Inter-Varsity Press, 1964), p. 23, writes, "[The Baptism of the Spirit] is, in fact, the means of entry into the body of Christ."
[5]Donald W. Dayton, "Holiness Movement, American," in *The New International Dictionary of the Christian Church*, ed. by J. D. Douglas (Grand Rapids: Zondervan Publishing House, 1974), p. 475.
[6]William W. Menzies, *Anointed to serve: The Story of the Assemblies of God* (Springfield, MO.: Gospel Publishing House, 1971), p. 27.
[7]Holdcroft, *The Holy Spirit*, p. 120.
[8]To cite but one example: Kilian McDonnell, "The Holy Spirit and Christian Initiation," in *The Holy Spirit and Power: The Catholic Charismatic Renewal*, ed. by Kilian McDonnell (Garden City, New York: Doubleday & Company, Inc., 1975), p.82.
[9]In spite of their separate titles—The Gospel of Luke and The Acts of the Apostles—and because Luke–Acts is a literary unit, the Gospel and the Acts are fundamentally the same literary genre.
[10]van Unnik, "Luke–Acts, A Storm Center in Contemporary Scholarship," p. 18.
[11]Hans Conzelmann, *The Theology of St. Luke*, trans. by Geoffrey Buswell (New York: Harper & Row, Publishers, 1960), p. 150.
[12]Conzelmann, *The Theology of St. Luke*, p. 150.

[13]Conzelmann, *The Theology of St. Luke*, p. 26.

[14]For a summary critique of Conzelmann's interpretation see W. Ward Gasque, *A History of the Criticism of the Acts of the Apostles* (Grand Rapids: William B. Eerdmans Publishing Company, 1975), p. 294, and Paul S. Minear, "Luke's Use of the Birth Stories," in *Studies in Luke–Acts*, p. 124.

[15]W. F. Lofthouse, "The Holy Spirit in the Acts and the Fourth Gospel," The *Expository Times* 52 (1940–41): 335.

[16]Lofthouse, "The Holy Spirit in the Acts and the Fourth Gospel," pp. 335–36.

[17]J. H. E. Hull, *The Holy Spirit in the Acts of the Apostles* (London: Lutterworth Press, 1967), pp. 68–69.

[18]Hull, *The Holy Spirit in the Acts of the Apostles*, p. 68.

[19]I. Howard Marshall, *Luke: Historian and Theologian*, Contemporary Evangelical Perspectives (Grand Rapids: Zondervan Publishing House, 1970), pp. 91; 93ff; 159ff; 170.

[20]Marshall, *Luke: Historian and Theologian*, p. 221.

[21]Holdcroft, *The Holy Spirit*, p. 110.

[22]Holdcroft, *The Holy Spirit*, p. 108.

[23]Carl Brumback, *"What Meaneth This" A Pentecostal Answer to a Pentecostal Question* (Springfield, MO.: Gospel Publishing House, 1947), p. 192; cf. pp. 198; 206.

[24]Holdcroft, *The Holy Spirit*, pp. 122–23.

[25]Frank Farrell, "Outburst of Tongues: The New Penetration," *Christianity Today* (September 13, 1963), p. 5.

[26]Stott, *The Baptism and Fullness of the Holy Spirit*, p. 8. This book went through eight American printings before it was issued as an expanded second edition in 1975.

[27]Stott, *The Baptism and Fullness of the Holy Spirit*, p. 18.

[28]For example, see recent discussion by Gordon D. Fee, "Hermeneutics and Historical Precedent—a Major Problem in Pentecostal Hermeneutics," in *Perspectives on the New Pentecostalism*, ed. by Russell P. Spittler (Grand Rapids: Baker Book House, 1976), and Ronald Kydd, *I'm Still There: A Reaffirmation of Tongues as the Initial Evidence of Baptism in the Holy Spirit* (Toronto: The Pentecostal Assemblies of Cananda, 1977).

[29]Kydd, *I'm Still There*, p. 11. Italics added.

[30]Marshall, *Luke: Historian and Theologian*, p. 56.

[31]Marshall, *Luke: Historian and Theologian*, p. 55.

[32]Martin Hengel, *Acts and the History of Earliest Christianity*, trans. by John Bowden (Philadelphia: Fortress Press, 1980), pp. 51–52.

[33]Hengel, *Acts and the History of Earliest Christianity*, pp. 41–42.

[34]Marshall, *Luke: Historian and Theologian*, p. 19.

[35]Marshall, *Luke: Historian and Theologian*, p. 52.

[36]Lofthouse, "The Holy Spirit in the Acts and the Fourth Gospel," p. 334.

[37]James Barr, *The Semantics of Biblical Language* (London: Oxford University Press, 1961), p. 222.

[38]Clark H. Pinnock and Grant R. Osborne, "A Truce Proposal for the Tongues Controversy," *Christianity Today* (October 8, 1971), p. 8. It is significant that by the time he reviewed Michael Green's *I Believe in the Holy Spirit*, *HIS* (June, 1976), p. 21, Pinnock had abandoned this methodological approach to the relationship between Luke and Paul.

[39]Dunn, *Baptism in the Holy Spirit*, p. 130.

[40]Dunn, *Baptism in the Holy Spirit*, p. 129.

[41]Stott, *The Baptism and Fullness of the Holy Spirit*, p. 23.
[42]Stott, *The Baptism and Fullness of the Holy Spirit*, p. 23.
[43]Dunn, *Baptism in the Holy Spirit*, p. 129.
[44]Green, *I Believe in the Holy Spirit*, pp. 141–42.
[45]Clark H. Pinnock, review of *I Believe in the Holy Spirit*, by Michael Green, in *HIS* (June, 1976), p. 21.
[46]Luke 1:15, 41, 67; Acts 2:4; 4:8, 31; 9:17; 13:9, 52, Ephesians 5:18.
[47]Stott, *The Baptism and Fullness of the Holy Spirit*, pp. 43–51.
[48]Marshall, *Luke: Historian and Theologian*, p. 75.

Chapter Two

[1]Francis Brown, S. R. Driver, and Charles A. Briggs, eds., *A Hebrew and English Lexicon of the Old Testament* (London: Oxford University Press, 1907), pp. 924–26; Henry George Liddell and Robert Scott, *A Greek-English Lexicon* (9th ed. with a Supplement; London: Oxford University Press, 1968), p. 1424.
[2]For an introduction to the charismatic movement see Richard Quebedeaux, *The New Charismatics: The Origins, Development, and Significance of Neo-Pentecostalism* (Garden City, New York: Doubleday & Company, Inc., 1976).
[3]R. Laird Harris, Gleason L. Archer, Jr., and Bruce K. Waltke, eds., *Theological Wordbook of the Old Testament*, Vol. II (Chicago: Moody Press, 1980), p. 837.
[4]Lloyd Neve, *The Spirit of God in the Old Testament* (Tokyo: Seibunsha, 1972), p. 124.
[5]Neve, *The Spirit of God in the Old Testament*, p. 129.
[6]Quoted from George Foot Moore, *Judaism in the First Centuries of the Christian Era: The Age of Tannaim*, Vol. I (New York: Schocken Books, 1971 repr.), p. 421.
[7]Neve, *The Spirit of God in the Old Testament*, p. 122.

Chapter Three

[1]The "we" passages are Acts 16:10–17; 20:5–21:18; 27:1–28:16.
[2]For a discussion of the "we" passages see the commentaries of F. F. Bruce, *The Acts of the Apostles: The Greek Text with Introduction and Commentary* (2nd ed., Grand Rapids: Wm. B. Eerdmans, 1952), pp. 2–3, and Ernst Haenchen, *The Acts of the Apostles: A Commentary*, trans. by Bernard Noble, *et al.* (Oxford: Basil Blackwell, 1971), pp. 489–91. I. Howard Marshall, *The Acts of the Apostles: An Introduction and Commentary*, The Tyndale New Testament Commentaries (Grand Rapids: Wm. B. Eerdmans, 1980), p. 263, responds to Haenchen: "Haenchen (pp. 489–91) argues that the reader would naturally suppose that one of the people just mentioned (Silas, Timothy) here begins to tell the story. This is highly unlikely; no reader would naturally suppose this, but would assume that the author of the book was including himself in the story."
[3]The story of Jesus has features in common with contemporary biographies, memoirs, and acts. Nevertheless, among the literary genre of New Testament times, the Gospel stands alone; it cannot be fully identified with any of these genre. For a brief discussion of

the problem see Ralph P. Martin, *New Testament Foundations: A Guide for Christian Students*, Vol. I: *The Four Gospels* (Grand Rapids: Wm. B. Eerdmans, 1975), pp. 15–29.

[4]In *Ecclesiastical History,* VI xiv. 6–7, Eusebius records the following testimony of Clement: "When Peter had publicly preached the word at Rome, and by the Spirit had proclaimed the Gospel, that those present, who were many, exhorted Mark, as one who had followed him for a long time and remembered what had been spoken, to make a record of what was said; and that he did this, and distributed the Gospel among those that asked him. And that when the matter came to Peter's knowledge he neither strongly forbade it nor urged it forward."

[5]Mark 12:36, Matthew 12:18, 28; 28:19.

[6]Luke 1:35; 3:16, 22; 4:1; 12:10, 12 and parallels.

[7]Luke 1:15, 17, 41, 67, 2:25–27; 4:1, 14, 18; 10:21, 11:13.

[8]G. Vermes, *The Dead Sea Scrolls in English* (revised ed.; Middlesex: Penguin Books, 1968), pp. 247–49. Deuteronomy 18:18–19 form part of a *Messianic Anthology* which also includes Deuteronomy 5:28–29, Numbers 24:15–17, Deuteronomy 33:8–11, and Joshua 6:26.

[9]George Foot Moore, *Judaism in the First Centuries of the Christian Era: The Age of Tannaim*, Vol. I (New York: Schocken Books, 1971 repr.), pp. 414–22, and Joachim Jeremias, *New Testament Theology, Part One: The Proclamation of Jesus* (London: SCM Press Ltd., 1971), pp. 76–82.

[10]Paul S. Minear, "Luke's Use of the Birth Stories," in *Studies in Luke–Acts*, ed. by L. E. Keck and J.L. Martyn (London: S.P.C.K, 1968), p. 116.

[11]Significantly, in the Gospel of John, Jesus is also the exclusive bearer of the Holy Spirit throughout His public ministry (1:32; 7:39; 16:7).

[12]E. Earle Ellis, editor, *The Gospel of Luke*, New Century Bible (London: Thomas Nelson and Sons Ltd., 1966), p. 91. See also Jeremias, *New Testament Theology*, p. 55, and Dunn, *Baptism in the Holy Spirit*, p. 33.

[13]C. K. Barrett, *The Holy Spirit and the Gospel Tradition* (new edition; London: S.P.C.K., 1966), pp. 41ff.

[14]Alfred Plummer, *A Critical and Exegetical Commentary on the Gospel According to St. Luke*, The International Critical Commentary: (5th ed., Edinburgh: T. & T. Clark, 1922), p. 107.

[15]Barrett, *The Holy Spirit and the Gospel Tradition*, p. 98.

[16]Quoted from F. F. Bruce, "The Spirit in the Apocalypse," in *Christ and Spirit in the New Testament*, ed. by Barnabas Lindars and Stephen S. Smalley (London: Cambridge University Press, 1973), p. 337.

[17]Martin McNamara, *Targum and Testament: Aramaic Paraphrases of the Hebrew Bible: A Light on the New Testament* (Grand Rapids: William B. Eerdmans, 1972), p. 41.

[18]McNamara, *Targum and Testament*, p. 45.

[19]Recent books on the subject of charismatic and prophetic leadership in the New Testament include the following: E. Earle Ellis, *Prophecy and Hermeneutic in Early Christianity: New Testament Essays* (Grand Rapids: William B. Eerdmans Publishing Company, 1978); Martin Hengel, *The Charismatic Leader and His Followers*, trans. by James Greig (New York: Crossroad, 1981); David Hill, *New Testament Prophecy*, New Foundations Theological Library (Atlanta: John Knox Press, 1979); Paul S. Minear, *To Heal and to Reveal: The Prophetic Vocation According to Luke* (New York: The Seabury Press, 1976), and David L. Tiede, *Prophecy and History in Luke–Acts* (Philadelphia: Fortress Press, 1980).

[20]Ellis, *The Gospel of Luke*, p. 8.

[21]Barrett, *The Holy Spirit and the Gospel Tradition*, p. 120.

Chapter Four

[1]Charles H. Talbert, *Literary Patterns, Theological Themes, and the Genre of Luke–Acts*, Society of Biblical Literature Monograph Series, 20 (Missoula: Scholars Press, 1974), p. 16.

[2]Contra Dunn, *Baptism in the Holy Spirit*, p. 54, who writes, "The Baptism in the Spirit [at Pentecost] as always, is primarily initiatory, and only secondarily an empowering."

[3]Not all accept this interpretation of tongues-speaking. For example, in his commentary on the Greek text of Acts F. F. Bruce proposes that what we have here is the disciples' being delivered from the peculiarities of their Galilean speech, p. 82. This interpretation fails to do justice to the bewilderment (2:6), amazement (2:7), and perplexity (2:12) of the crowd, or to the charge of drunkenness (2:13).

[4]Contra Hull, *The Holy Spirit in the Acts of the Apostles*, pp. 68–69.

[5]Howard M. Ervin, *"These Are Not Drunken, As Ye Suppose"* (Plainfield, New Jersey: Logos International, 1968), pp. 79–87.

[6]Eric G. Jay, *New Testament Greek: An Introductory Grammar* (London: S.P.C.K., 1958), p. 166.

[7]Ernest de Witt Burton, *Syntax of the Moods and Tenses in New Testament Greek* (3rd ed.; Edinburgh: T. & T. Clark, 1898), p. 16.

[8]Quoted from C. K. Barrett, editor, *The New Testament Background: Selected Documents* (New York: Harper & Row, Publishers, 1961), p. 157.

[9]Eduard Lohse, "πεντηκοστη," in *Theological Dictionary of the New Testament*, VI, ed. by Gerhard Friedrich, trans. by Geoffrey W. Bromiley (Grand Rapids: Wm. B. Eerdmans, 1970), p. 49.

[10]Theodor H. Gaster, *Festivals of the Jewish Year* (New York: Sloan Associates Publishers, 1952), p. 71. He writes: "To this Christian version of Pentecost, Judaism now opposed its own. Not the Church, but the community of Israel had been founded on that day. Not to a select few, but to a whole people had come the revelation of God. Not over the heads of favored disciples had the tongues of fire appeared, . . . *all the people* saw the thunders and the flames (Exod 20:18). . . . God Himself had spoken in a multitude of tongues; for, so the sages asserted, every word uttered from the mountain had been pronounced in seventy-two languages at the same time."

[11]Leon Morris, "Resurrection," in *The New Bible Dictionary*, organizing editor, J. D. Douglas (Grand Rapids: Wm. B. Eerdmans, 1962), p. 1087.

[12]These examples are from G. Ernest Wright, *The Book of the Acts of God: Contemporary Scholarship Interprets the Bible* (New York: Doubleday & Company, Inc., 1957), pp. 21–22.

[13]Conzelmann, *The Theology of St. Luke*, p. 95.

[14]Dunn, *Baptism in the Holy Spirit*, pp. 51–54.

[15]Jacob Jervell, *Luke and the People of God: A New Look at Luke–Acts* (Minneapolis: Augsburg Publishing House, 1972), p. 15.

Chapter Five

[1]Dunn, *Baptism in the Holy Spirit*, p. 55.

[2]Dunn, *Baptism in the Holy Spirit*, pp. 63–68.

[3]Dunn, *Baptism in the Holy Spirit*, p. 68.

[4]In Acts the term "disciples" always describe the disciples of Jesus, that is, Christians. At Ephesus Paul found "some" disciples. Some interpreters believe that Luke uses the indefinite pronoun here to distinguish between the regular company of disciples and this group. Yet Luke uses the same pronoun in the singular to describe Ananias as a "certain" disciple (Acts 9:10). He also describes Timothy as a "certain" disciple (Acts 16:1). Thus, whether in the singular or in the plural, the indefinite pronoun describes the disciples of Jesus.

[5]Dunn, *Baptism in the Holy Spirit*, p. 88.

[6]George Eldon Ladd, *A Theology of the New Testament* (Grand Rapids: William B. Eerdmans, 1974), pp. 345–47. See also E. Schweizer, "πνευμα, πνευματικος" in *Theological Dictionary of the New Testament*, VI, ed. by Gerhard Friedrich, trans. by Geoffrey W. Bromiley (Grand Rapids: William B. Eerdmans, 1968), pp. 413–15.

[7]Stephen S. Smalley, "Spirit, Kingdom and Prayer in Luke–Acts," *Novum Testamentum* XV (1973): 68.

[8]Hull, *The Holy Spirit in the Acts of the Apostles*, p. 90.

[9]Schweizer, "πνευμα," *TDNT*, VI, p. 414.

[10]Michael Green, *Evangelism in the Early Church* (Grand Rapids: William B. Eerdmans, 1970), p. 149.

Chapter Six

[1]Harold Hunter, "Spirit Baptism in Luke–Acts" (unpublished seminar paper, Fuller Theological Seminary, 1975), pp. 17ff.

[2]A. M. Stibbs and J. I. Packer, *The Spirit Within You: The Church's Neglected Possession*, Christian Foundations (London: Hodder and Stoughton, 1967), p. 33; Leon Morris, *Spirit of the Living God: The Bible's Teaching on the Holy Spirit* (London: Inter-Varsity Press, 1960), pp. 63ff.

[3]Stott, *Baptism and Fullness*, pp. 33, 48–49, 68.

[4]Dunn, *Baptism in the Holy Spirit*, p. 54; Stott, *Baptism and Fullness*, p. 71.

FOR FURTHER READING

Barrett, C. K. *The Holy Spirit and the Gospel Tradition.* New edition. London: S.P.C.K., 1966.

Bruner, Frederick Dale. *A Theology of the Holy Spirit: The Pentecostal Experience and the New Testament Witness.* Grand Rapids: William B. Eerdmans, 1970.

Carter, Charles Webb. *The Person and Ministry of the Holy Spirit: A Wesleyan Perspective.* Grand Rapids: Baker Book House, 1974.

Dunn, James D. G. *Baptism in the Holy Spirit: A Re-Examination of the New Testament Teaching on the Gift of the Spirit in relation to Pentecostalism today.* Studies in Biblical Theology. Second Series, 15. London: SCM Press Ltd., 1970.

_____.*Jesus and the Spirit: A Study of the Religious and Charismatic Experience of Jesus and the First Christians as Reflected in the New Testament.* New Testament Library. London: SCM Press Ltd., 1975.

Ervin, Howard M. *"These Are Not Drunken, As Ye Suppose."* Plainfield: Logos International, 1968.

Ewert, David, *The Holy Spirit in the New Testament.* Scottdale: Herald Press, 1983.

Green, Michael. *I Believe in the Holy Spirit.* Grand Rapids: William B. Eerdmans, 1975.

Holdcroft, L. Thomas. *The Holy Spirit: A Pentecostal Interpretation.* Springfield: Gospel Publishing House, 1979.

Horton, Stanley M. *What the Bible Says About the Holy Spirit.* Springfield: Gospel Publishing House, 1976.

Hull, J. H. E. *The Holy Spirit in the Acts of the Apostles.* London: Lutterworth Press, 1967.

Hummel, Charles E. *Fire in the Fireplace: Contemporary Charismatic Renewal.* Downers Grove: Inter-Varsity Press, 1978.

Lampe, G. W. H. *God As Spirit: The Bampton Lectures, 1976.* Oxford: Oxford University Press, 1977.

_____.*The Seal of the Spirit.* Second edition. London: S.P.C.K., 1967.

McDonnell, Kilian, ed. *The Holy Spirit and Power: The Catholic Charismatic Renewal,* Garden City: Doubleday & Company, Inc., 1975.

Montague, George T. *The Holy Spirit: Growth of a Biblical Tradition.* New York: Paulist Press, 1976.

Moody, Dale. *Spirit of the Living God: The Biblical Concepts Interpreted in Context.* Philadelphia: The Westminster Press, 1968.

Morris, Leon. *Spirit of the Living God: The Bible's Teaching on the Holy Spirit.* London: Inter-Varsity Press, 1960.

Neve, Lloyd. *The Spirit of God in the Old Testament.* Tokyo: Seibunsha, 1972.

Palmer, Edwin H. *The Person and Ministry of the Holy Spirit: The Traditional Calvinistic Perspective.* Grand Rapids: Baker Book House, 1958.

Sanders, J. Oswald, *The Holy Spirit and His Gifts.* Contemporary Evangelical Perspectives. Grand Rapids: Zondervan Publishing House, 1970 repr.

Schweizer, Eduard. *The Holy Spirit.* Translated by Reginald H. and Ilse Fuller. Philadelphia: Fortress Press, 1980.

Stibbs, A. M., and Packer, J. I. *The Spirit Within You: The Churches Neglected Possession.* London: Hodder and Stoughton, 1967.

Stott, John R. W. *Baptism and Fullness: The Work of the Holy Spirit Today.* Second edition. London: Inter-Varsity Press, 1975.

Swete, Henry Barclay. *The Holy Spirit in the New Testament.* Grand Rapids: Baker Book House, 1976 repr.

Wood, Leon J. *The Holy Spirit in the Old Testament.* Contemporary Evangelical Perspectives. Grand Rapids: Zondervan Publishing House, 1976.

INDEX OF SCRIPTURE REFERENCES

93